Ask Bethany

FAQs: Surfing, Faith & Friends

Other books in the Soul Surfer Series:

Soul Surfer Bible

Fiction:
Clash (Book One)
Burned (Book Two)
Storm (Book Three)
Crunch (Book Four)

Nonfiction:
Rise Above: A 90-Day Devotional

Ask Bethany

FAQs: Surfing, Faith & Friends

Bethany Hamilton
with Doris Rikkers

zonder**kidz**

ZONDERVAN.com/
AUTHORTRACKER
follow your favorite authors

ZONDERKIDZ

Ask Bethany
Copyright © 2007 by Bethany Hamilton

This title is also available as a Zondervan ebook.
Visit www.zondervan.com/ebooks.

Requests for information should be addressed to:
Zonderkidz, *Grand Rapids, Michigan* 49530

Library of Congress Cataloging-in-Publication Data

Hamilton, Bethany.
        Ask Bethany : FAQs : surfing, faith & friends / By Bethany Hamilton with Doris
Rikkers.
            p.   cm.
        ISBN 978-0-310-72568-8 (softcover)
        1. Hamilton, Bethany — Religion — Juvenile literature. 2. Christianity — Miscellanea —
Juvenile literature. 3. Girls — Religious life — Juvenile literature. I. Rikkers, Doris. II. Title.
BR124.H36 2010
248.8'2 — dc22   2010038310

Art direction: Merit Alderink
Cover design: Merit Alderink
Interior design: Christine Orejuela-Winkelman

Printed in the United States of America

11 12 13 14 15 /DCI/ 24 23 22 21 20 19 18 17 16 15 14 13 12 11 10 9 8 7 6 5 4 3 2 1

Contents

A Word from Bethany

To everyone who has asked me nicely, begged me, or pleaded for me to ple-e-a-s-e write back—here it is.

To the hundreds of you who have been kind and wonderful and said great things to encourage me since I lost my arm in a shark attack in 2003—here are my replies to your emails, letters, questions, and comments that I could never have managed to answer separately (so-o-o sorry!). But if I ever even tried to read and answer all the letters and emails and questions that I get every day, I'd be writing 24/7!

Try to think of this book as the best of me to you.

Love,

Bethany

Bethany Basics

Q. It has been a long time since I have seen your picture. What do you look like now?

Q. How tall are you?

A. I'm taller now than I was when I was attacked by the shark. I was 5'7" when I was 13, but now I'm 5'10". I have blond hair and hazel eyes and an Irish–Norwegian heritage.

Q. How old are you?

A. I'm 20 years old now.

Q. When is your birthday?

A. I was born February 8, 1990.

Q. Where do you live?

A. I live in the town of Princeville, on the north shore of the island of Kauai, in the state of Hawaii, in the middle of the Pacific Ocean.

Q. Were you born in Hawaii or someplace else?

A. I was born in Hawaii, on the island of Kauai, in the emergency room at Wilcox Memorial Hospital.

Q. Where do you go to school?

A. I now stay home to go to school—that sounds funny, doesn't it? Anyway, I went to Hanalei Elementary School in the town of Hanalei, on Kauai. I started homeschooling after sixth grade so I'd have more time to surf. I do my studies through American School. They have students all over the world! I pretty much *have* to homeschool these days because I travel so much.

Q. Are you a Christian?

A. Yes, I am. I believe in Jesus Christ as my Lord and Savior and my God. I have a personal relationship with God through Jesus Christ. For more about my faith see the chapter "About Faith."

Q. When did you become a Christian?

A. I've been a Christian for as long as I can remember. I was about five when I recognized Jesus as my Savior and committed to follow him, love him, and live my life for him!

Q. Where do you go to church?

A. I go to the North Shore Community Church near my home.

Q. What color is your hair?

A. I have medium length, straight blonde hair. It looks just like my mom's hair did when she was my age.

Q. I heard you have blonde hair. Is that your natural color? Do you use peroxide or anything on it?

A. My hair is thin, so it naturally bleaches out from the sun even more than most people's hair. I like everything real and natural, so I don't use artificial products and I try to avoid chemicals as much as possible.

Q. I heard you're really cute, so I checked out some of the pics on the Web. Sure enough, you are. Life's not fair. How come you're cute and popular, and I'm not?

A. God makes us the way we are for a reason and he never makes a mistake. You were designed with his perfect love! We just have to make the best of what we've got. And besides, it's what's inside us that really counts. Kindness and love are more important than looks. My mom has me look up words in the Strong's Concordance to find their deeper meaning. I found out that real beauty is more valuable if it's inside our hearts. *Grace, pleasant, agreeable, precious, delight, honor,* and *godly* were a few of the words that were a part of being beautiful. Sin is what really makes a person look ugly, so be beautiful with a clean heart!

On the Same Wave

Here's what the Bible tells us about outward appearance:

The LORD said to Samuel, "Do not consider his appearance or his height... The LORD does not look at the things man looks at. Man looks at the outward appearance, but the LORD looks at the heart."

—1 Samuel 16:7

Beauty is more about what's on the inside than what's on the outside.

Your beauty should not come from outward adornment... Instead, it should be that of your inner self, the unfading beauty of a gentle and quiet spirit, which is of great worth in God's sight."

—1 Peter 3:3–4

Q. What's your middle name?

A. Meilani, which means "heavenly flower."

Q. Do you have a nickname, or does everybody call you Bethany?

A. Bebo, B-ham, or Bethy.

Q. What's your favorite holiday?

A. Valentine's Day.

Q. Who's your favorite movie star?

A. I don't really have one, but I like to laugh, so I'd say either John Heder, who plays Napoleon Dynamite, or the actor who plays Dewey in *Malcolm in the Middle*.

Q. Do you have any pets? If yes, what are their names?

Q. What kind of pets do you have?

A. I have a dog, a shar-pei named Ginger. She's the most adorable little dog you'll ever see! She's been in our family for years. I used to have a horse named Koko. My mom sold her because she took too much time away from surfing, and she bucked too much.

Q. Do you take your pets with you when you travel?

A. No. Ginger hates water, so she doesn't like to go to the beach. We even had to get her a raincoat so we could walk her. (It rains a lot here.)

Q. Who takes care of your dog when you're gone?

A. There's usually somebody in my family still back at home—my dad or one of my brothers. My entire family doesn't come along when I travel. So someone is home to take care of things, including my dog.

Q. Do you have your driver's license?

A. Yes, I have my driver's license! In the summer of 2006 I finally passed the test, and now I can drive myself to the beach and Bible study!!!

Q. I hear you've tried snowboarding. What do you think of it?

A. I really liked it. Snowboarding is a lot like surfing waves because they both require good balance. Turning on a snowboard is the opposite of how you turn on a surfboard, though. When you turn on a snowboard, you use your front foot to pivot. In surfing you use your back foot. Every time I go back to surfing waves after snowboarding, I have to change my thinking. I'm a bit mixed up, and it takes a wave or two to get comfortable surfing again.

Q. Do you do any other extreme sports other than surfing?

A. An extreme sport is usually life threatening and very dangerous. I don't consider surfing an extreme sport unless you are going out in twenty-plus-foot waves. I tried bungee jumping in Thailand, which did not make my mom happy, but I loved it!

Q. What advice would you give somebody facing challenges?

A. No matter what kind of challenge you face—emotional, physical, or social—the advice is the same: Always ask God for help, guidance, and inspiration! He can open doors that you would never think or dream of! When you make Jesus the first priority in your everyday life, he can help you overcome obstacles and face challenges. Don't give up. Keep working hard.

Sometimes you need to change your focus to other things, something more doable. I played the ukulele in elementary school and then switched to guitar, and now I just play my iPod because I am more focused on my surfing. My mom wants me to learn the keyboard because I love music so much. But I am really too busy to do that. I hope some of you will take up where I left off with my music skills. That would make me smile! With God's help you can do anything according to his will, so get on your knees and pray. Seek out his great plan for your life, and he will never let you down! Nothing is impossible for God.

On the Same Wave

Here's what the Bible says about nothing being impossible for God:

Ah, Sovereign LORD, you have made the heavens and the earth by your great power and outstretched arm. Nothing is too hard for you.

—Jeremiah 32:17

No eye has seen, no ear has heard, no mind has conceived what God has prepared for those who love him.

—1 Corinthians 2:9

Jesus looked at them and said, "With man this is impossible, but not with God; all things are possible with God."

—Mark 10:27

Q. What do you do for fun?

A. Hawaii is hot, so I enjoy spending a lot of time in the water. I like to snorkel and look for shells in the water with friends. This summer the waves haven't been too abundant, so my friends and I have been learning to play tennis. We also help out with the junior high Bible study group, which gets pretty crazy but is lots of fun! I love cooking, and this last year I have been learning new recipes from TV, friends, and family. I have been having great fun with my friends learning to cook healthy food. Then we bring it to Bible study and make everyone eat it! Yikes! I really enjoy reading a good book too!

Q. Do you ever feel that what happened has ruined your life? If I lost an arm, I think my life would be ruined.

A. I don't see my life as ruined. Everybody has to face some difficulties in life. I have met people who are missing both arms. That is an incredible challenge! I have a neighbor who is quadriplegic, and he runs his own business. A bitter heart is more of a handicap than any physical setback.

Q. How would you describe your life before the attack and now?

A. Before the attack I'd say my life was busy with school, surf contests, fun with friends, and lots of church youth group activities.

Then there was the attack. Now things are kind of in the category of wild and crazy. My life is full of opportunities to be a witness for Jesus, to help others, and still keep my passion for surfing alive. I just keep praying and trusting that God will show me which things to choose so that I can tell others about his love and all he's done in my life. All for his glory and honor!

Q. You always have cute swimsuits on in your pictures. Where do you like to shop?

A. All of my bathing suits are supplied by my sponsor, Rip Curl. They have great suits and send me lots to choose from. I need suits that are functional out in the water, as a surfing wipeout can have a bad effect on a weak suit!

Q. How long have you been surfing?

A. I started surfing on my own when I was five. So I've been surfing about fifteen years now.

Q. I'm ten and have no idea what I want to be when I grow up. Did you know what you wanted to do at my age?

A. Yes, I wanted to be a professional surfer. But most people don't know what they want to do when they're ten, so don't worry about it. While you're growing up, enjoy the things that you like and do them as well as you can. Try different things so you can find out what works for you and what you really like to do and excel at. I like the same things now that I liked when I was younger. And I love Jesus more now than ever, especially as I get older and get to know him more and more over years of answered prayers and guidance. It is so exciting to learn to trust in Jesus and know he is always there for you. Trust him to guide you with your future! Think about what you do that makes you happy. That might be a clue as to what you should do when you grow up. And ask God to show you what you're good at.

Q. Do you have any hobbies?

A. Cooking, art, and photographing flowers.

Q. What's your favorite color?

A. I have a few, really: blue (like the ocean), orange and pink (like a sunset), and green (like the mountains on Kauai). Every color is special, and my favorites can change from time to time.

Q. Do you really have saltwater in your veins? I read that somewhere.

A. I have blood in my veins like everyone else. "Saltwater in your veins" is an expression that means "I've grown up and love being in, on, and near the ocean and the waves."

Q. What's your favorite food?

A. I love eating healthy food. Smoothies are one of my favorites. I practically live on them. Papaya and acai fruit smoothies are the best! I also love ahi tuna salads and chicken lettuce wraps!

Q. Do you like junk food?

A. I eat dark chocolate and sweets once in a while, but not much. I always try to eat healthy food, like fruits and veggies. It's important to have a healthy balanced diet, especially since I'm an athlete and want to be strong to surf.

Q. Do you exercise every day?

A. I like to exercise every day. I keep varying what I do so I don't get bored. I really enjoy running with my iPod and with a friend or two. Running builds my lungs so I can hold my breath under water longer. I do sit-ups to strengthen my stomach, as it helps with twisting and turning while riding your surfboard. When I travel, I use the workout rooms. If it's rainy, I still surf—unless the conditions aren't safe. For the most part, I try to surf every day even if the conditions are not good. Many contests don't have perfect waves, and you have to be ready for anything.

On the Same Wave

Here's what the Bible says about our bodies:

Do you not know that your body is a temple of the Holy Spirit, who is in you, whom you have received from God? You are not your own; you were bought at a price. Therefore honor God with your body.

—*1 Corinthians 6:19–20*

Therefore, I urge you, brothers, in view of God's mercy, to offer your bodies as living sacrifices, holy and pleasing to God—this is your spiritual act of worship.

—*Romans 12:1*

Q. Do people stare at you 'cause you only have one arm?

A. Most people recognize me unless I really cover up; but that is hard to do in Hawaii because it's hot. Little kids tend to look because they really don't know anything about me. But most people are gracious and polite.

Q. Would you rather have people stare and whisper about your missing arm or ask you straight out, "Where'd your arm go?"

A. I think most people recognize me from hearing my story on TV, so they don't need to ask. Sometimes a little kid will ask where my arm went. I don't mind, because I get to have some fun and make up a wild, funny story about how I lost the arm!

Q. Does it bother you having only one arm?

A. I have to make many adjustments in my everyday life. Some things are frustrating and I have to ask for help, like putting my hair up in a ponytail. Some people don't survive their shark attacks, so I don't feel sorry for myself. I try not to forget that I could have died in a flash!

Q. Are you thinking about getting a fake arm?

A. A fake arm is called a prosthetic. A company called Hanger Orthopedics made a prosthetic arm for me; it was an amazing process. I had to dip my right arm into amalgam—the stuff that is used to form fake teeth. Then they reversed the design to be like my left arm. The fingernails on it can hold nail polish, and I look pretty cool wearing it! It is too nice to wear in the water or at the beach, which is where I am every day, so I usually leave it home.

On the Same Wave

**If we have one arm or two,
if our arms are weak or strong,
God's arms will be stronger and always
ready to protect us. Here's what the
Bible says about God's arms:**

*O LORD God Almighty, who is like you? You are mighty,
O LORD, and your faithfulness surrounds you.... Your
arm is endued with power; your hand is strong, your
right hand exalted.*

—Psalm 89:8, 13

*The eternal God is your refuge, and underneath are
the everlasting arms.*

—Deuteronomy 33:27

Q. Do you ever feel sorry for yourself?

A. Feeling sorry for myself is a choice that I try not to make. That would not please God or bring him honor. He has been too good to me for me to make selfish choices. I'm happy that I am alive and can still surf. I'm still able to do almost everything I could do with two arms, so I have no reason to pity myself. God's Word teaches us to be thankful in every situation in life and to use our challenges to glorify him! So I realize that he has given me this opportunity to help others in their walk with God and to share his good news of salvation.

Q. Do you do any other sports besides surfing?

A. I enjoy snowboarding a lot. But I usually have to go to the mainland to find snow, so I can't do that too often. I like soccer, horseback riding, and skateboarding. Recently, my friends and I have been learning to play tennis for fun, and we are taking ju jitsu classes too! I really like to do a lot of different things just for fun.

Q. Do you like to watch TV? What's your favorite TV show?

A. I really don't watch TV much. But if I'm home, I like to watch the Food Network. *The Planet's Funniest Animals* is a blast to watch! I like to learn about interesting things on the Discovery Channel. And on the Christian Television Network, this show called *Bananas* can be pretty funny. Another show called *Virtual Memory*, which tests your Bible skills, is fun to watch. My friends and I try to outguess the contestants and the host on that show—it is hilarious!

Q. Who is the greatest influence in your life?

A. Jesus Christ and my parents!

Q. Do you have a role model? Who?

A. Jesus is my main role model. My youth leader, Sarah, is amazing too! She is beautiful, and she surfs and likes to have fun. She deeply loves the Lord and is an incredible role model for my youth group and me.

Q. What is your typical day like?

A. I don't know if I have a typical day anymore. There's so much going on: travel, speaking engagements, and competitions. But if I'm not traveling, my day might look like this: I'm up early and make my bed. I usually make a smoothie for breakfast, feed Ginger, and then head to the beach to check the surf. If the surf is good, I surf. If it's too flat, I'll go home to do schoolwork and get in some other kind of physical activity. Late in the afternoon I try to surf again. In the evening, I may do homework, hang out with friends, eat dinner with the family, or read a good book. I have a great Bible study group, so I go to that in the evenings a few nights a week. We always plan to do something fun and special on the side, usually on Friday night.

At some point in the day, I make time to read my Bible and spend time talking and listening to God. If anyone has offended me or hurt my feelings, I make sure to deal with it as it comes up so I can stay open with God and understand what he expects of me.

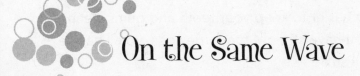

On the Same Wave

**Reading God's Word and talking
to him keeps us near to him.
Here's what the Bible says about
being close to God:**

Come near to God and he will come near to you.

—James 4:8

*I have hidden your word in my heart that I might
not sin against you.*

—Psalm 119:11

*Seek the LORD while he may be found; call
on him while he is near.*

—Isaiah 55:6

*Oh, how I love your law! I
meditate on it all day long.*

—Psalm 119:97

Q. I noticed you had braces. Do you think I should get them?

A. I wore braces for a couple of years. My teeth now look so much better. I just got them off, and now my teeth are straight and perfect. If you have crooked teeth or a messed-up bite, then braces are probably a good idea. It's easier to keep your teeth and gums clean when you have straight teeth. Besides, you'll have a beautiful smile!

Q. I have to get braces next month. I heard it hurts. Does it?

A. It does hurt a little. It hurts just after the orthodontist tightens the wire, but it's not that bad. You might need to eat soft food for a day. I recommend drinking smoothies. And after a while, you'll be good to go!

Q. Do kids make fun of you when you have braces?

A. Nobody has made fun of me that I know of. Good friends will be encouraging and not laugh. The kids who like to make fun of others probably do it just to make themselves look cool. Just pray for them and move on, remembering your end goal—a beautiful smile!

Q. How long did you have your braces?

A. I started wearing braces when I was fourteen. I had to wear them for about three years. I was so excited to get them off so I could look pretty; and then I landed face first on the reef while surfing and had to deal with a huge scar and scabs on my chin!

Q. Do you like working with two arms or one better?

A. When you lose an arm, you have a serious revelation on how amazing God is with his talent of designing the human body. How incredible the design is of two hands and arms and the whole balance of the human body. We were definitely not made by accident! There are a whole lot of things that are easier to do with two arms, but I don't have that option anymore. One arm is better in an odd sort of way, 'cause now I have the chance to tell a whole lot of people about Jesus and the strength, love, and hope he offers. If I still had two arms, I wouldn't have been able to tell so many people about finding hope in Jesus' plan.

Q. Do you believe in miracles?

A. Definitely! I know that some people think that God did miracles in the Bible and then stopped. But he didn't stop. God performs miracles every day. And I'm one of them. It was a miracle that I'm here to tell about the shark attack. Check out the details in the chapter "Shark Attack!" The most valuable miracle is a heart that has been changed by the love of Jesus!

Q. How can you afford to fly all over the place?

A. Most of the time my airfare and expenses are paid by the people who are asking me to go someplace to speak or to do something. My parents still have to pay for some of the expenses for my surfing competitions, but my sponsor, Rip Curl, helps out with that too.

Q. Do kids in other countries know about you? If they don't, they should.

A. My book *Soul Surfer* has been translated into other languages and sold in other countries. And my story was on the news in other countries too. Kids in some countries know about me 'cause I've gone there to see them—like the kids in Japan, Germany, and England. The kids in Thailand, where the tsunami hit, know me 'cause I went there to talk to them and encourage them to go back into the water. Playing in the water has its own special form of healing.

My book is popular in Australia and New Zealand, so people must know about me there too. I also have gotten emails from people in Central and South America, Canada, and Africa. I guess, really, the answer to your question is yes. Kids in other countries do know my story and are hearing about how I love Jesus.

Q. Do people from other countries write to you?

A. Oh, yeah. People from all over the world write me letters and emails. I've gotten mail from all over the United States, New Zealand, Australia, Austria, Japan, England, Switzerland, France, Central and South America, Canada, Africa, and Spain—to name just a few. I don't keep track of all the places. If you like geography, look all those up on your map and learn about all the special places God has made.

Q. I'm twelve and want to be a gymnast in the Olympics. What advice would you give me?

A. Good for you to have such a great goal! In order to succeed, you will need a lot of support from your parents and coaches. You have to be willing to work hard. But go for it! You never will know if you can succeed until you try. You can also use your skills to teach other kids when you get older. I've thought about teaching surfing to kids when I get older, and I probably will once in a while. Remember, ninety-five percent of your success comes from hard work and practice.

Q. What's the most fun thing you've ever done?

A. That's not an easy question. Bungee jumping was pretty fun, but that's up there with getting a really good barrel in surfing.

Q. I'm afraid of lots of stuff, like the dark and thunderstorms. Are you afraid of anything?

A. Sharks, snakes, and spiders give me the creeps. Fear can be a very good thing! It can protect you from danger and from doing something that you shouldn't. It can protect you from getting bit by a snake or washed away in a flood. I have learned through the Word of God about how deep his love is for each of us. He will take care of us according to his will. Sometimes he will allow difficult things to happen to us in order to draw us closer to him and to help us live a better life with real meaning and purpose.

Q. How often do you get to the mainland?

A. I usually get to the mainland at least four or five times a year for various surf contests (Southern California), snowboarding (Colorado, California, Utah, or Idaho), and other appearances all over the States. It is not easy traveling all of the time, and if I weren't doing it for Jesus, I would stay at home. We are called to be his hands and his feet and tell others about his wonderful love.

Q. If you could wish for anything, would you wish to have two arms again?

A. I never wish for anything because I believe in the power of prayer! Growing up, I experienced so many answered prayers from a real and living God. My mom has raised me to have a life of prayer. It is a very cool way to live your life; knowing that you have an awesome God that loves you and cares for you and watches over you, protecting you as he sees fit and using you in his own special way! Losing my arm was not the worst thing that could have happened to me, and a lot of good has come out of it.

Q. How has the attack changed you?

A. I look at life a little differently than I did before. I guess that's true for a lot of people who survive an attack. I know that I'm very glad to be alive. And I thank God for that. I am also very grateful that I can still surf. Being alive and being able to surf makes me very thankful. When you come to a point in your life where you really truly want to serve and follow God on a seriously deep level, God won't let you down!

I am more deeply committed in my love for Jesus and take my relationship with him more seriously than ever. I realize that God loves everyone sooooooo much, and that he is always looking for a voice to share about his love. I have definitely had to get very real and serious about my walk with God and had to decide if I am really real in my commitments to serve and obey him.

On the Same Wave

Here's what the Bible says about being thankful:

Give thanks to the LORD, for he is good. His love endures forever.

—Psalm 136:1

Always [give] thanks to God the Father for everything, in the name of our Lord Jesus Christ.

—Ephesians 5:20

Give thanks to the LORD, call on his name; make known among the nations what he has done.

—1 Chronicles 16:8

Thanks be to God for his indescribable gift!

—2 Corinthians 9:15

Give thanks in all circumstances, for this is God's will for you in Christ Jesus.

—1 Thessalonians 5:18

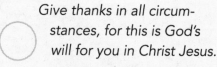

Q. Do you ever surf the Web?

A. Since I'm so busy with so many other things, I don't have a lot of time to surf the Web. When I do, I'm pretty careful where I go and what I look at. I like to stay in touch with my friends through email. And sometimes I use the Internet for research and to check the surf forecast and reports.

Q. In all your pictures, you are always smiling. What makes you so happy?

A. Jesus! Christ lives in me and fills my heart with joy when I need it. I am not always smiling, especially if I am tired, but those pictures get edited! It is usually sin and lack of forgiveness that can spoil your heart, so I try to keep a clean heart so I can smile! That's why I'm so happy.

On the Same Wave

**God is the source of our happiness.
Here's what the Bible says about joy:**

The joy of the LORD is your strength.
—Nehemiah 8:10

May all who seek you rejoice and be glad in you; may those who love your salvation always say, "Let God be exalted!"
—Psalm 70:4

May the righteous be glad and rejoice before God; may they be happy and joyful.
—Psalm 68:3

You have made known to me the paths of life; you will fill me with joy in your presence.
—Acts 2:28

Be joyful always.
—1 Thessalonians 5:16

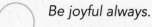

Q. I just finished reading *Soul Surfer*. I loved your book. It's awesome. What made you write it?

A. So many people wanted to hear about my story that I (with a lot of help from friends and family and a writer) decided to write it all down. I really wanted to tell everyone what God had done for me and how he cares for me—that my faith in him got me through and gave me courage. And above all, I wanted to tell them that Jesus loves everyone.

Q. How long does it take to read your book?

A. It really depends on how fast you read, I guess. Some adults have read it in two hours. Kids have read it in one night or two to three days. But everyone agrees it's a fast read. And it was designed to be so.

Q. Did a lot of people read your book?
Q. How many people have read your book?

A. People are still reading it. There are over 350,000 copies in print. And when it was first out, it even made the *Los Angeles Times* bestseller list. (That's a big deal, I guess.) I know that some of the copies went to libraries, and then a whole bunch of kids probably read from the same copy. Some kids have written emails to tell me they've read the book twice. A few readers have even read it over six times!

Q. Are you glad you wrote the book?

A. Yes. I've been amazed how many people have read it and liked it. I know that a lot of kids have been encouraged by the book to keep going toward the dreams they have set their heart on. I hope that some people have come to know Jesus through my story. I want readers to know that God loves them and can do great things in their lives.

Q. How can I find out more about you?

A. Oh, there are lots of ways. You can continue reading this book, read my book called *Soul Surfer*, go to my website bethanyhamilton.com, or watch my movie when it comes out.

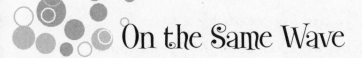

On the Same Wave

All kinds of books are written every day. There are a lot of great books that we could read. But the greatest book in the world is God's book — the Bible.

As for God, his way is perfect; the word of the LORD is flawless.

—2 Samuel 22:31

Your word is a lamp to my feet and a light for my path.

—Psalm 119:105

Jesus answered, "It is written: 'Man does not live on bread alone, but on every word that comes from the mouth of God.'"

—Matthew 4:4

Shark Attack!

Q. When were you attacked by a shark?

A. On October 31, 2003, about 7:00 in the morning.

Q. Where did it happen?

A. Off the north shore of Kauai, Hawaii, at a surf spot called Tunnels.

Q. Why didn't you pick a different beach?

A. Originally my mom and I were headed to a place called Pauaeaka, but when we got there the waves were just too small. While heading home, we stopped to check out the surf at Tunnels, and I ended up going out when my friends showed up.

Q. Had there been sharks in that area before?

A. Yes. There have been shark sightings all over Kauai, even at Tunnels. There had been complaints of a shark harassing surfers in that area, but we had not heard that report.

Q. What were you thinking when it happened?

A. It happened so fast, but I remember knowing exactly what was happening. I felt my board lift and sudden pressure on my left arm. I saw a flash of gray as I was jerked side to side—and I knew it was a shark! But even as soon as I thought that, it was over. I knew exactly what had happened, but couldn't believe it had happened to me.

Q. What did you do when you realized a shark had bit you?

A. Right after the shark let go of me and vanished, I called out to my friend Alana and her dad and brother. "I just got bit by a shark."

Q. Did you scream?

A. I guess I was in shock or something. I didn't scream.

Q. Weren't you completely terrified?

A. I know that would be a normal reaction, but I don't remember being terrified. Two weeks before, I had taken a lifeguard emergency-response training class and had learned how important it is not to panic. But I know that it was God's peace that kept me calm that day.

Q. Weren't you afraid the shark would come back and eat you alive?

A. I don't even think that crossed my mind. Sharks don't like to eat people. Also, to get back to shore, I had to paddle across a reef that was too shallow for a shark to follow.

Q. Were you lying on your surfboard or sitting on it?

A. I was lying down, relaxing in the water with my right hand on the nose of the board and my left hand dangling in the water.

Q. Did you see the shark swimming toward you?

A. No. I didn't know anything was in the water near me, no less a shark. Although you know subconsciously that there is sea life beneath you.

Q. Did the shark glare at you and give you the "hairy eyeball" before taking a bite?

A. No. Nobody in the water saw it coming. I just saw a gray blur slip back into the water. I'm so glad that God spared me the trauma of seeing the shark before it bit me, so I don't have horrible nightmares for the rest of my life.

Q. Did it hurt?

A. No. I only felt pressure and a tug on my arm when it was biting me. I've heard that when the body goes into survival mode, it can turn off the pain reaction in order for you to do what you have to do to survive.

Q. Did you get blood all over your bathing suit? Was it ruined?

A. I have a bloody towel for a souvenir, but my suit was clean of blood by the time I got to the beach.

Q. Did you see the shark that attacked you?

A. I never saw the shark. All I remember seeing was a big gray blur. I guess it was good that I didn't see how big it really was. That might have freaked me out even more.

Q. How big was the shark?

A. It was about fourteen and a half feet long.

Q. Is the shark still out there?

A. No. The shark is dead. After the attack, two guys went hunting for the shark. Ralph Young and Billy Hamilton caught it and brought it back to shore. The jaws matched the teeth marks on the hunk taken out of my surfboard.

Q. Do shark attacks happen often in Hawaii?

A. No. Hawaii has very few shark attacks. Shark attacks happen the most off the coast of Florida. Most shark attacks are minor.

Q. Do sharks really eat people?

A. No. Sharks don't eat people. They eat fish, sea birds, and seals. They also eat dead fish and other sea animals to keep the ocean clean. Their menu doesn't include people. Sometimes they mistake people for seals or something they do eat. After one bite of a human, a shark usually lets go.

Q. Was it your right arm or your left arm?

Q. Are you right-handed or left-handed?

A. I'm right-handed. I lost my left arm in the attack.

Q. Don't people usually die from a shark attack?

A. Not all the time. Most shark-attack victims just need a few stitches. Some people die from blood loss. My blood loss was really bad. I could have died, but God didn't want me to. He saved me.

Q. Why do you think you survived the attack?

A. This is kind of a mystery to a lot of people. I think God saved me. He kept me calm, and it certainly helped that I was in good physical shape. According to the doctors, most people who die from a shark attack die from loss of blood, panic, or from bad infections caused by bacteria in the mouth of the shark. I lost over fifty percent of my blood, but I still made it.

Q. Were you out there all alone? If you were, that wasn't a smart thing to do.

A. I wasn't alone. My friend Alana was with me. Her brother Byron and her dad, Holt, were with us too. You are right. It's always smart to surf with a buddy. I almost always do. Most surf spots tend to be overcrowded, so surfing alone is usually not an issue.

Q. Were you wearing any jewelry?

A. I was just wearing a watch on my left arm. Surfers usually wear a watch to keep track of the time and how long they've been surfing. I use a watch to time my competition heats. It's easy to lose track of time when you're doing something you love!

Q. Are sharks attracted to jewelry?

A. Sharks aren't necessarily attracted to jewelry, but they are attracted to shiny objects. A watch like mine can look like an eyeball of a fish. Sharks are attracted by blood. They can smell blood from miles away. Surfers know that if they get cut up on the reef or by a surfboard fin, they need to head for shore and call it a day.

Q. I want to start surfing, but I'm afraid of sharks and other stuff in the water. What should I do?

A. Don't get caught up worrying about it. If you swim in a lake or the ocean, there are going to be live creatures swimming around—that's where they live. They're not interested in you. You have a better chance of getting a bee sting than getting bit by—or even seeing—a shark. Shark attacks are extremely rare.

Q. How long did the shark stick around?

A. The attack only lasted about three seconds. Then the shark swam away. I don't know if it stuck around because we got out of there as fast as we could.

Q. How did you swim back to shore?
Q. How did you get back to shore?

A. I didn't have to swim. I was lying on my surfboard when Holt, Alana and Byron's dad, saw a wave coming and pushed me into it. Byron, Alana's brother, paddled alongside and caught the wave with me. Together we rode the wave on our bellies across and to the end of the reef. Then I traded boards with Byron so I could use his board, which had better flotation because it didn't have a bite out of it. He took my board and paddled ahead to the beach to call 9–1–1. Next, we had to paddle over a deep channel to get to the beach. Holt had me grab his board shorts as he paddled me in tow to the beach.

Q. Were there people around to help you?

A. Since I was surfing with Alana and her dad and brother, I had lots of help from them. Then when we got to the beach, there were other people that helped out, including a paramedic who happened to be renting a vacation rental right there. He was great to have around to oversee everything; he made us feel more at ease in spite of the situation.

Q. Did Alana scream when she saw the blood?

A. She was pretty much in shock. I know she was crying.

Q. How did the people surfing with you react when they saw you were missing an arm?

A. My friends Holt, Byron, and Alana Blanchard were shocked when I told them a shark attacked me. And Byron said he had to do a double take when he saw my arm was gone. Without a second thought, though, Holt jumped into action and told everyone what to do to get me to the beach as fast as possible. Everybody managed to stay calm and focused on getting me back to shore and getting help. But Alana cried hard and threw up when we got to the beach. We were the only ones surfing in the area at that time.

Q. Do you remember any part of getting back to the beach?

A. I remember most of it. What I remember most is praying over and over, "Please God, help me. Let me get back to the beach." I remember thinking for a second, "I wonder if I will lose my sponsors?" I also remember Holt taking off his long-sleeve rash guard that he was wearing and wrapping it around my arm as a tourniquet to help stop the bleeding. He kept telling me to keep talking to him and Alana. So I prayed out loud.

On the Same Wave

Here's what the Bible says about prayer:

The LORD has heard my cry for mercy; the LORD accepts my prayer.

—Psalms 6:9

Let us then approach the throne of grace with confidence, so that we may receive mercy and find grace to help us in our time of need.

—Hebrews 4:16

This is the confidence we have in approaching God: that if we ask anything according to his will, he hears us. And if we know that he hears us—whatever we ask—we know that we have what we asked of him.

—1 John 5:14–15

Q. Did you pass out?

Q. Did you go unconscious after the shark bit you?

A. No. I only remember parts of that trip back to the beach, but I never passed out. I kept talking to Holt and praying, but I don't remember anything specific I said. I was able to stay conscious the whole time. Good thing, or I might have fallen off my board and drowned.

Q. How long did it take you to get back to the shore?

A. Twenty minutes.

Q. How did you stop from bleeding out all your blood?

A. My friend's father, Holt Blanchard, used his rash guard as a tourniquet while we were still in the water. Later he replaced it with a surf leash as a tourniquet to stop the bleeding.

Q. Were you in really deep water when it happened?

A. Yes, I was a long way out from the beach. It was about a quarter of a mile—over two reef shelves.

Q. Where were your mom and dad?

A. My mom was back home after dropping me off to surf for the morning. My dad was at the hospital getting ready to have routine knee surgery.

Q. Did your mom come and take you to the hospital?

A. My mom was back at home, and it would have taken her even longer than the ambulance to get me to the hospital. She drove straight to the hospital instead.

Q. Who called 9-1-1?

A. Byron paddled in ahead of us, got to the beach, and called.

Q. Where were the lifeguards? At our beach the lifeguards make you get out of the water if they see a shark.

A. The lifeguards weren't on duty yet. It was too early in the morning.

Q. Were there other people on the beach to help you?

A. There were other people who came to help. Paul Wheeler, who is a paramedic in California, came down from his beach house and checked me out. Other people brought beach towels to try and keep me warm. Jeff Walba donated his surf leash to use as a better tourniquet on my arm, and he called my mom.

Q. Did the shark wreck your surfboard?

A. Yes. The shark took a huge bite out of my board.

Q. Was your dad mad that your surfboard got wrecked?

A. No. He didn't care about my surfboard. He was mad at the shark for hurting me.

Q. What happened to the surfboard from the attack?

A. We've used it in a lot of photo shoots to give people an idea of how big a bite the shark took. We will probably put it in the surf museum in California.

Q. Was the ambulance on the beach to take you to the hospital?

A. It was about forty minutes before the ambulance got to the beach. It had to come from the town, and nobody can go really fast down the winding roads.

Q. Did they sound the sirens and go really fast to get you to the hospital?

A. The road on the north shore of Kauai is a winding road, so it's hard to go real fast. I don't remember the sirens, but I suppose they used them to get me to the hospital as fast as possible. Other friends reported hearing the sirens.

Q. What was it like to ride in an ambulance?

A. I only remember parts of it. I remember getting stuck with needles and being put on a stretcher and slid into the ambulance. I also remember the paramedic saying to me softly, "God will never leave you or forsake you." He knew my parents and had attended the same church years earlier.

Q. How long did it take to get you to the hospital?

A. It seemed like forever. It was long enough—about forty-five minutes.

Q. How did your mom find out?

A. Jeff Walba, the guy whose surf leash was used as a tourniquet, called my mom from his cell phone.

Q. Were the doctors nice to you?

A. Everyone in the hospital was very nice to me. Dr. Ken Pierce knew me from church and from the surfing scene. (He's a surfer too.) Dr. Rovinsky was the orthopedic surgeon who was going to operate on my dad's knee. (He's a surfer too.) I had nurses around all the time who were very caring and friendly. As I got better, I had a physical therapist and then an occupational therapist help me get back to normal. Everyone was great and very caring and concerned.

Q. Why didn't the doctors sew your arm back on?

A. Doctors can sometimes reattach an arm after an accident if it's available. But my arm was gone. The shark took it. I had what they call "a traumatic amputation."

Q. Did they ever think that you might die?

A. The idea crossed everybody's mind; it was definitely a concern. Because of the amount of blood loss, I could very easily have slipped away. But everyone was working hard to save my life. That was the real important thing to focus on. My arm was already gone, so they needed to make sure that the wound was perfectly clean so that it didn't get infected. Later, I had a second surgery to close the wound, using a flap of skin from under my armpit.

Q. Did you have to wear a cast?

A. No, I think casts are mostly used to heal broken bones. The doctors stitched me up and covered the stitches with lots of gauze and tape.

Q. Did they give you blood in the hospital?

A. Yes. They had to give me a blood transfusion since I had lost so much of my own blood.

Q. Did you get a lot of flowers and cards and gifts for being in the hospital?

A. There were so many flowers around that I thought it looked like a miniature version of the garden of Eden. I remember that it smelled great—more like a garden than a hospital. Every time I woke up, there was another bunch of balloons floating over my bed. And after a while, the teddy bears started taking over!

Q. Were your friends allowed to come to see you?

A. You couldn't stop them. There were all kinds of people visiting me: friends of my parents, friends from church, lifeguards and the beach community, and lots of people I didn't even know. On that Sunday, the entire youth group from Kauai Christian Fellowship and the North Shore Community Church showed up. We had a little worship service and prayed together. It was great! Since I couldn't get to church, the church came to me! When I started feeling better, my friends came and hung out with me. We started clowning around and even played some jokes on the nurses.

On the Same Wave

Here's what the Bible says about worshiping God:

Therefore, since we are receiving a kingdom that cannot be shaken, let us be thankful, and so worship God acceptably with reverence and awe, for our "God is a consuming fire."
—Hebrews 12:28–29

Come, let us bow down in worship, let us kneel before the LORD our Maker; for he is our God and we are the people of his pasture, the flock under his care.
—Psalm 95:6–7

Worship the LORD with gladness; come before him with joyful songs. Know that the LORD is God. It is he who made us, and we are his; we are his people, the sheep of his pasture.
—Psalm 100:2–3

Q. How long did you have to stay in the hospital?

A. I had to stay there six days. At first I was so tired that the time didn't matter. Then as I started getting better, I got bored and the days seemed really long. The IV machines that drip medicine into your arm were noisy, so it was hard to sleep. I was really eager to get out of there and go home.

Q. While you were in the hospital, were you depressed?

A. God gave me peace about the whole thing so I didn't really get depressed at all. I felt confident that God would take care of everything. That everything would work out okay. I was alive and that is what we were focused on. Many shark victims die from infections because sharks' mouths are very dirty with bad bacteria. So I was happy to be alive!

On the Same Wave

God promises us peace. Here's what the Bible says about peace:

You will keep in perfect peace him whose mind is steadfast, because he trusts in you.

—Isaiah 26:3

[Jesus said,] "Peace I leave with you; my peace I give you. I do not give to you as the world gives. Do not let your hearts be troubled and do not be afraid."

—John 14:27

I will listen to what God the LORD will say; he promises peace to his people, his saints.

—Psalm 85:8

[Jesus said,] "I have told you these things, so that in me you may have peace. In this world you will have trouble. But take heart! I have overcome the world."

—John 16:33

Do not be anxious about anything, but in every-thing, by prayer and petition, with thanksgiving, present your requests to God. And the peace of God, which transcends all understand-ing, will guard your hearts and minds in Christ Jesus.

—Philippians 4:6–7

Q. How did the newspapers and TV people find out about your story?

A. News travels fast, especially when everyone knows everybody else on a small island. News of a shark attack also spreads like wildfire in a surfing community. So eventually someone on the local newspaper found out, and word just got out from there. More than a few people have police radios and hear what is going on immediately. We were personal friends with Guy Hagi, a surfer and news reporter, and he did my first interview. It was good to have a friend to talk to instead of a stranger. In just a few days there were all kinds of news people outside the hospital eager to get the full story. It was pretty overwhelming for my family.

Q. How did your family react when they heard you had been attacked by a shark?

A. When my mom heard on the phone, she didn't believe at first. Later, on the way to the hospital, she broke down and cried. My brother Noah jumped out of bed when my mom told him. He flew into action and called prayer teams and some family friends, but he was breathless and terrified when he told them the news. My dad was ready for knee surgery when a nurse told the doctor that a thirteen-year-old girl was coming in due to a shark attack and they would need the operating room for her. My dad knew that the girl had to be me or Alana. When he found out it was me, his heart dropped. He said he felt helpless because he couldn't be by my side—his legs were numbed from the spinal tap. My brother Tim was at Kapaa High School in the library when he got the call from Noah. He hung up on him, left school, and raced to the hospital.

Q. What kind of shark was it? Was it a great white?

A. It was a tiger shark.

Q. Did you lose a lot of blood?

A. Yes, tons. I lost over fifty percent of the blood in my body. Most people die from losing that much blood. I had to get a blood transfusion! I believe God wanted me to live, and allowed me to beat the odds.

Q. How big a bite did the shark take?

A. I lost ninety percent of my arm—all the way up to the shoulder. And it took a big eighteen-inch bite out of my surfboard too.

Q. Did you cry?

A. Yes, I did cry. Not right away. But I cried in the hospital after the doctor removed the stitches and told me I would have to wait another five days before I could go into the ocean. The tiny stitch holes needed to close before I could go in. Losing an arm takes some getting used to. Not being able to surf was the most painful.

Q. What kept you going while you were in the hospital and having surgery?

A. I got my strength to keep going from my relationship with Christ and from the love and encouragement of my family and friends. Everyone was so great. I could feel God's love coming through all of them, expressed in their loving care. God showed me that he had a purpose for my life, and this would be a big part of it.

On the Same Wave

Here's what the Bible says about God's strength and purpose:

"For I know the plans I have for you," declares the Lord, "plans to prosper you and not to harm you, plans to give you hope and a future."

—*Jeremiah 29:11*

God is our refuge and strength, an ever-present help in trouble.

—*Psalm 46:1*

So do not fear, for I am with you; do not be dismayed, for I am your God. I will strengthen you and help you; I will uphold you with my righteous right hand.

—*Isaiah 41:10*

The Lord stood at my side and gave me strength, so that through me the message might be fully proclaimed.

—*2 Timothy 4:17*

Q. Do you have nightmares?

A. I have had more than a few nightmares about sharks. At first I cried, but my mom got up and prayed with me, and I could go back to sleep.

Q. When you see yourself in your sleep, do you have one arm or two?

A. Two. The mind remembers everything, and I sometimes even have feeling in the arm that's gone. Isn't that weird?

On the Same Wave

Here's what the Bible says about sleep:

When you lie down, you will not be afraid; when you lie down, your sleep will be sweet.

—Proverbs 3:24

I will lie down and sleep in peace, for you alone, O LORD, make me dwell in safety.

—Psalm 4:8

I lie down and sleep; I wake again, because the LORD sustains me.

—Psalm 3:5

Q. What did you want to be before you got bit by the shark? Did the attack make you change your mind?

A. I've wanted to become a professional surfer since I was eight. For a little while when I was in the hospital after the attack, I thought I wouldn't be able to ever surf again. That didn't last long. I have a deep passion for surfing, and I was determined to keep going—arm or no arm. And I did; with God's help.

Q. Did you ever think that you might never surf again?

A. The day after the attack, I started thinking about becoming a surf photographer instead. And I remember saying something about switching to soccer. But the next day when I was starting to feel better, I quickly changed my mind. I was sure that I would be able to get back on my board again. I already missed surfing and was itching to get back in the water.

Q. Did your mom and dad have any worries about you surfing again?

A. They are surfers too and know the kind of passion I have for the sport. They understand completely that I have to do this. But they are still concerned about sharks and are pickier about where I surf.

Q. What was it like getting back on your board the first time after your attack?

A. My family didn't plan for me to surf so soon—doctor's orders. I was just going to sit on the beach and watch my friends surf. It was the day before Thanksgiving. I got so anxious and excited because all of my friends were out and the waves were really fun, I just had to get in the water. So I called my family, and they came down to the beach. I paddled out on a longboard with my family and friends right there with me. It felt weird paddling with only one arm, and it was a lot harder than I expected. My dad offered to push me into the waves, but I said I wanted to do it on my own. So I finally paddled into a wave, caught it, tried to stand up, but tipped my board. This happened again, and my dad noticed what was happening. He told me to put my hand in the center of my board as I pushed to stand up so the board wouldn't tip to the side. So I tried again with that in mind, and I got up! It was my third wave, and I rode it all the way into the beach! I had tears of happiness because I was so stoked to be out there again and able to surf!

Q. I've heard people say that your story is inspiring. How can a story of a shark bite be inspiring?

A. It's not the story itself that's inspiring. It's the results and the meaning behind it all: my reaction to losing an arm and how God turned a tragedy into triumph. I actually won first place in a national surf competition in California in 2005, an achievement I had been attempting for years!

Q. Do you get tired of telling the shark attack story?

A. It can be hard to answer the same questions over and over. That is why I had to write the first book, *Soul Surfer*. I really want people to understand the meaning of the story—not just the facts about the attack and all that went on. God did miraculous things for me that day. *He* should be the focus of the story, not the shark or me.

Q. Have you ever surfed Tunnels since the attack?

A. A couple of times. I didn't plan on ever surfing there again, but the waves were good and my friends were going out so I just went with the flow!

Q. Do you believe in miracles?

A. The whole ordeal was one big miracle when you add up all the many little details. The fact that I stayed calm was partly due to the lifeguard class I had taken two weeks earlier. God knew what was ahead. Surfers have many times used surf leashes for tourniquets in other situations. Alana's dad, Holt, was the right person to be with at the time because he can keep calm in an emergency, and he knew what to do. I see a lot of the details as God's plan and guidance. To me, a miracle is the evidence of the marvelous handiwork of God. My entire story is a string of miracles, showing that God was in control of every event and detail that happened that day and the days following.

On the Same Wave

God is a god of miracles. Here's what the Bible says about miracles:

I will remember the deeds of the LORD; yes, I will remember your miracles of long ago. I will meditate on all your works and consider all your mighty deeds.

—Psalm 77:11–12

[God] performs wonders that cannot be fathomed, miracles that cannot be counted.

—Job 9:10

You are the God who performs miracles; you display your power among the peoples.

—Psalm 77:14

Look to the LORD and his strength; seek his face always. Remember the wonders he has done, his miracles, and the judgments he pronounced.

—1 Chronicles 16:11–12

Q. What do you feel and think now about the attack as you look back on it?

A. Looking back, I'm glad that the shark didn't attack someone else out there that day. I can see that my getting attacked by that shark was for a purpose—it was no mistake or coincidence. I think it was a good thing (even though it is so hard to say that). God is and was in control of my life, and I would want it no other way. I trust him completely—even more now that I've seen what he can do when I have faith in him!

How Do You Do That?

Q. Right after the attack, did you constantly think, "How will I do that with one arm?"

A. My doctor, Dr. Rovinsky, said, "The list of what you will have to do differently is long; the list of what you won't be able to do is short." I decided early on that he was right and started learning to do things on my own. One by one.

Q. Is it difficult to do some things with just one arm?

A. Yes. But even in the hospital, right after the attack, a therapist showed me how to do lots of things with just one hand. I was amazed at how they had that all figured out. You can do a lot of things one-handed if you practice. I try to live simpler by wearing clothes that don't have complicated clasps, ties, or zippers and shoes that have Velcro instead of strings—simple details that just happen to be in style!

Q. I'm a surfer. How do you surf with only one arm? You're amazing! I know I could never do it.

A. I was pretty scared about whether I'd be able to paddle hard enough to catch waves and be able to stand up on the board, but I guess my passion and strong desire to surf again just pushed me. My dad and my brother Noah have come up with some clever ideas to help me.

I now use customized boards that are longer and thicker than before to help with paddling. Noah has been a huge help in getting me to progress to more high-performance, innovative designs. Boards in general get beat up pretty fast, and Noah keeps me surfing on the cutting edge of board designs that will work for me. My dad created a strap on the top middle of my board that helps me to push under waves while paddling out. And now I position myself deeper and catch waves a little later than other people.

Q. How do you braid your hair with only one hand?

A. I use my mouth to ask my mom or friends nicely to please braid or put my hair in a bun or ponytail. Even my brother Timmy is pretty good at helping me out!

Q. How do you blow-dry your hair?

A. I usually let my hair air dry the natural way. But if I'm in a big hurry and have to get somewhere fast and look my best, someone else (like my mom or a friend) will blow-dry it for me. I *can* do it myself, but it looks better if I have a little help.

Usually I let it air dry because it is warm here in Hawaii, and wet hair keeps you cool!

Q. Can you cut your own food up or does somebody have to do that for you?

A. I can cut my own food. I learned how to do that too. One gift that I received was a knife-fork combo that is pretty fun to use! Sometimes I ask my mom to cut for me—like in a restaurant. I rarely eat meat, and it is usually not too hard to cut veggies.

Q. How do you open a bottle of pop?

A. I don't drink soda; it's not good for your health. On rare occasions I get a Blue Sky soda from the health-food store or an IZZE, which is fruit juice and sparkling water, but I mostly drink purified water or fruit juice. But if I have to open a bottle, I sit down, prop it between my knees or feet, and open it with my right hand. Or if I'm standing up, I put the bottle between my legs to hold it tight and then open it. Cans with pull tabs are much easier.

Q. How do you peel an orange?

A. At first, I would hold the orange between the soles of my feet and peel it with my hand. I'd do the same with a tangerine or a banana. But now, I just ask for help or use my knees or teeth, because it's not very sanitary to touch the food with your feet!

Q. How do you tie your shoes?

A. In the hospital, the therapist taught me a new way to tie shoes, but I'm not very good at it. I usually wear slip-on or Velcro shoes or rubber slippers (flip-flops). Or, as with my running shoes, I just ask someone to tie them for me and then I leave the strings tied.

Q. How do you button buttons? I tried it with one hand and gave up. It's too hard.

A. When you have to, you figure those types of things out. Some clothes are designed "easy to wear" so I buy those, and I avoid buying clothes with lots of buttons or that are difficult to get on. Tank tops and T-shirts work for me. Some things you can't really avoid—like jean pants. They usually have at least one button. Swimsuits don't ever have buttons, and I wear those a lot. Actually, I have my mom pre-tie my swimsuits and then I just slip them over my head!

Q. How do you keep your spirits up? 'Cause I know I have my dark days when I'm feeling down since my accident.

A. Making choices is a daily thing each of us has to do. We can choose to follow Jesus and obey him and have peace in our lives. We can choose to help others and not hang out in the negatives. There are so many good things that God has given us to do. Only he can fill our hearts with his joy!

Q. How do you stay so positive and have such a good attitude? I'd be so bummed if I lost an arm.

A. I read and hear every day that people die in car accidents and other tragedies. I have life and I have Jesus! Feeling sorry for yourself will only make you and everyone around you sad and miserable. It is okay to feel down sometimes. It's just better to think positive and use what you have to the fullest potential.

My parents taught me how to handle losing and winning with the right attitude. They taught me to always pray when I have a bad attitude and to ask God to change my heart and thoughts. In those times, God shows me a lot through his Word.

More than anything, God's principles and wisdom have helped me handle losing my arm. I couldn't do it without God's Word in my heart and his Spirit living in me. His words, promises, purpose, and plan for my life are what keep me positive.

On the Same Wave

Here's what the Bible says about the kind of attitude we should have:

Since Christ suffered in his body, arm yourselves also with the same attitude, because he who has suffered in his body is done with sin. As a result, he does not live the rest of his earthly life for evil human desires, but rather for the will of God.

—1 Peter 4:1–2

Rejoice in the Lord always. I will say it again: Rejoice! Let your gentleness be evident to all. The Lord is near.

—Philippians 4:4–5

Whatever is true, whatever is noble, whatever is right, whatever is pure, whatever is lovely, whatever is admirable—if anything is excellent or praiseworthy—think about such things.

—Philippians 4:8

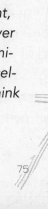

Q. Is there any thing that you can't do?

A. There is one thing that I don't do very well with only one arm—play guitar. It used to be one of my favorite things to do, but now I am helping my brother Tim learn, and that is fun!

Q. I have so much stuff to carry to school that I need both arms. How do you carry your books to school?

A. Well, I don't go to a school campus. I study right at home, so I don't have to lug my books around. But if I have lots of stuff to carry, I usually use a backpack and carry it over my shoulders so I have a free hand to carry something else.

Q. How do you wear a ski jacket? Can you zip it up?

Q. How do you zip up your coat?

A. If I had to, I could zip a jacket up on my own, but it takes a long time, and I get frustrated if it is taking too long. So, my mom helps me or other people do. I always go to the mountains with family or friends, never alone. Living in Hawaii, I don't have to wear a coat or jacket very often. But if I'm visiting a cold climate or am snowboarding, then I do have to wear a ski jacket. I wear a jacket just like everyone, but I just let one sleeve hang. Sometimes we get North Winds in Hawaii, which tend to be cold, but I just slip a pullover sweatshirt over my head.

Q. Are you afraid of sharks?

A. I think we all are. Fear can save your life
and help you make good decisions. Part
of me says that it can't happen twice.
Sharks don't come around that much.
Once is weird; twice won't happen. If you
want to surf, you just need to use wisdom
in the choices that you make. Don't surf
near fishermen who have just chummed
the water (thrown fish or corn overboard
to attract fish). Don't surf a river mouth
after a heavy rain, as sharks feed off the
downstream debris, and so on.

Q. How do you type with only one arm?

A. I type with one hand. I don't go as fast as other people, but I can get by. There is a keyboard designed for one hand where the letters are placed in a better position, but I just make due with the everyday keyboard so if I travel I am comfortable with what is commonplace.

Q. How do you stay calm and focused when you surf? I'd be freaking and would constantly worry about another shark.

A. I stay focused on the waves and how stoked I am whenever I ride a wave. Trusting God means not worrying, so I decide to trust him, and if I feel uneasy then I go back to shore. I have done that a few times.

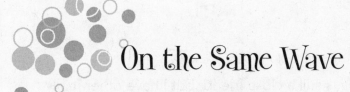

On the Same Wave

**Here's what the Bible says about
God protecting us and keeping us safe:**

*The LORD protects the simplehearted; when I was in
great need, he saved me.*

—Psalm 116:6

*He guards the course of the just and protects the way
of his faithful ones.*

—Proverbs 2:8

Keep me safe, O God, for in you I take refuge.

—Psalm 16:1

Friends and Family

Q. Do you have a lot of friends?

A. Yeah, I do!

Q. Is Alana still your best friend?

A. Yes, Alana is still a close friend, but I have other really close friends too!

Q. If Alana surfs in the same competitions that you do, don't you feel bad if she does better than you do?

A. Alana and I enjoy competing against each other. We make it fun. It doesn't hurt our friendship. I push and challenge and encourage her, and she does the same for me. We're pretty tough on each other and it makes us better surfers.

Q. How did your friends react to your attack?

A. They were as shocked as anyone else. They heard I lost my arm, and they were bummed—thinking I wouldn't be able to surf anymore—but supportive. A lot of them had just gotten into surfing when they turned thirteen. They cried at the hospital, but they actually made me laugh and brightened up my day. They entertained me at the hospital and as I recovered at home.

Q. You said your friend Alana was with you. How did she handle seeing you bleed?

A. The shark bit me and left a pool of blood in the water, but as soon as Alana's dad got the tourniquet on, there wasn't too much more real bleeding going on—it just trickled. Alana was pretty freaked! I think she cried on the paddle to the beach. She stayed alongside me to make sure that I didn't pass out or fall off the board. Once on the beach, she threw up! To be honest, I don't really remember too many details of what she did. I guess I was too focused on getting to the beach. I remember her yelling to her dad to get help. She was a little nervous about going surfing again after it happened. The first time she did, she thought she spotted another shark, but it was just a sea turtle.

Q. How do your friends feel about you being famous?

Q. Do your friends still like you now that you're famous?

A. To my friends, being "famous" really just means that I am gone a lot. It is hard to travel so much and not be around for our regular routine. But my friends were already kind of used to me traveling for surf contests. My friends are great. Even though I do all this stuff and travel a lot, when I come home they treat me like normal. It is so good to just be me when I'm with them. Sometimes I tell them what I've been up to, but if I don't want to talk about it and just want to surf or goof around or something, they're cool about it.

Q. Have you ever played a team sport like basketball?

A. One of my friends lives next door to a basketball court, so we shoot hoops just for fun! Nothing formal though. Soccer is big here in Hawaii, and it is a good way to make friends. I started playing soccer in first grade. It was a great learning experience. I've learned that every position in soccer is as important as another. Everybody needs to do their best at their job to help the team win. I played soccer all through grade school and really enjoyed being part of a team.

Q. When my friends say mean and nasty things about me, what should I do?

A. Pray! Jesus taught us to pray for our enemies! Even people close to us can act like an enemy would. Spend time with God and ask him for wisdom to heal the relationship. Jesus had friends who failed him, so he can understand what you're going through. If your friends just made a mistake and didn't know what they were saying, you should tell them that they hurt your feelings. Then you need to forgive them and forget about it! Too many friendships end because friends hold a grudge and won't forgive each other. It is not easy to find good friends, and they are worth their weight in gold.

On the Same Wave

Here's what the Bible says about forgiving others:

And when you stand praying, if you hold anything against anyone, forgive him, so that your Father in heaven may forgive you your sins.

—Mark 11:25

Make sure that nobody pays back wrong for wrong, but always try to be kind to each other and to everyone else.

—1 Thessalonians 5:15

Forgive whatever grievances you may have against one another. Forgive as the Lord forgave you.

—Colossians 3:13

Peter came to Jesus and asked, "Lord, how many times shall I forgive my brother when he sins against me? Up to seven times?" Jesus answered, "I tell you, not seven times, but seventy-seven times."

—Matthew 18:21–22

Q. My friend is going out with a guy behind her parents' backs. They think she is too young to date, but she's going out anyway. What do you think she should do?

A. She should stop lying to her parents. Her parents might have a very good reason why they don't want her to date. She should probably talk to them about it; she needs to know what the rule is all about. Maybe her parents would be okay with group dating. My brothers were in a youth group that had so much fun together going out in groups of girls and guys. They also made commitments through the True Love Waits ministry.

Q. Do you like boys?

A. Yes, but I believe God has perfect timing, and I want to wait for my true love. I just keep them as friends right now—nothing more.

Q. Do you have a boyfriend?

A. No. God fulfills my need for love right now. I believe a boyfriend is a dangerous thing and could change the course of your life overnight!

Q. Do you think kissing a boy is okay?

A. No! Kissing is giving a part of yourself to someone else. It carries a lot of weight in a relationship. I don't think it should be just a casual thing. Any kind of physical interaction makes you more emotionally attached to a person. Here's an example: Take two different colors of paper that represent a girl and a boy. When those two people get physical in their relationship, even if it's just holding hands, those two pieces of paper get stapled together. Every time they hold hands or kiss, one more staple binds them together. Then if the girl and boy break up, those pieces of paper get torn apart. Pieces of each paper get stuck to the other paper. Since the boy and girl were attached to each other, it hurts when they are separated. Parts of their hearts were given to each other. I really believe that we should wait to date boys and get involved in those ways until we are old enough to love and commit to another person.

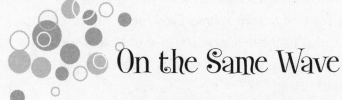

On the Same Wave

Here's what the Bible says about true love:

Love is patient, love is kind. It does not envy, it does not boast, it is not proud. It is not rude, it is not self-seeking, it is not easily angered, it keeps no record of wrongs. Love does not delight in evil but rejoices with the truth. It always protects, always trusts, always hopes, always perseveres. Love never fails.

—1 Corinthians 13:4–8

Be devoted to one another in brotherly love. Honor one another above yourselves.

—Romans 12:10

Q. Do you live with your mom and dad?

A. Yes. I'm very blessed to have a mom and a dad who are still married to each other. Their names are Cheri and Tom. My mom knows God led them to be together and that there is no luck in the Bible. God's provision, blessings, and tender loving care are pretty hard to beat!

Q. What was your life like when you were younger?

A. I was raised on the beach. With two energetic little boys, my mom went to the beach every day, and I was the tagalong baby. I have been going to surf contests since I can remember. We went to church every week, and at home we had the *Kids Sing Praise* videos, so I grew to love contemporary worship music at a young age. My favorite music video had zoo animals!

Q. What does your father do for a living?

A. My dad works as a professional waiter at a fine dining restaurant in a big hotel here on Kauai. He's kind of my manager now too, along with my brother Noah. He handles my schedule and stuff.

Q. What does your mom do?

A. Before our lives changed, she was a banquet waitress for conventions at the same hotel my dad works at. She's good at being a mom. She spends lots of time now traveling with me. When I didn't drive, she was the one who would cart me around to places to surf, to see my friends, and to church events. And she's my greatest prayer support. My mom does as the Bible says: she "prays without ceasing."

Q. Do you have a sister? I do. But she's too little to do anything.

Q. Do you have brothers?

A. I don't have any sisters—that is why I enjoy my friends so much! But I have two brothers: Tim and Noah. They're both a lot older than I am. They are both great photographers. Noah shoots digital still photography, and Tim shoots digital video and is working on his second body-boarding video.

Q. What do your brothers do?

A. Tim is an avid body boarder. He wanted to turn pro, but there is not enough money in the tour to make it professionally. For him to make videos works out really well, and he is very good at it! Noah does photography for a living and is my manager (along with my dad).

Q. What are your brothers like?

A. Noah is the boss, and Tim does what he says!

Q. Do you have other family—like cousins and aunts and uncles and grandparents?

A. Yeah; my extended family is spread out across the mainland. My dad's family lives in New Jersey. My mom's family lives in California.

Q. Does your family surf?

A. My mom used to surf, and she even competed. She doesn't surf that much anymore. But my dad goes surfing with me sometimes. My brother Noah is a standup surfer like me. Tim likes to body board.

Q. Does anyone else in your family compete in surfing contests?

A. No. I'm the only one who competes now. My mom and dad have both competed occasionally. My brothers competed at a lot of kids' contests when they were young. Every once in a while they compete in a contest.

Q. What's your family like?

A. My family is great. We are all very close. We all love
the Lord, and we love surfing. We love each other very
much and can pray together as well as goof around
together. We are not always perfect and can get tired
and grumpy with each other. But the Holy Spirit helps
us to stay on track. We love to play practical jokes and
have a good time. Our family motto is "The family that
surfs and prays together stays together." Amen!

Q. My parents are so strict. They are unreasonable
and drive me crazy. Why should I listen to them?
They never listen to me.

A. Ask God to help you with this. Ask God to help you
listen and to help your parents listen. My mom and
dad are great, but I don't always understand the
reason behind a rule. If I don't know, I try to ask them
before I get upset. Think of one time your parents
were unreasonable that bothers you the most. Practice
what you will say to them from your point of view and
without yelling. When you are ready, go talk to your
parents about it. Listen to what they have to say. Our
parents are usually trying to protect us from getting
hurt now or in the future. Even if you don't agree with
them, the more we obey our parents, the more they
will trust us to do things we want to do.

On the Same Wave

Here's what the Bible says about kids and parents:

Children obey your parents in the Lord, for this is right. "Honor your father and mother"—which is the first commandment with a promise—"that it may go well with you and that you may enjoy long life on the earth."

—Ephesians 6:1–3

Children obey your parents in everything, for this pleases the Lord.

—Colossians 3:20

Listen, my son, to your father's instruction and do not forsake your mother's teaching. They will be a garland to grace your head and a chain to adorn your neck.

—Proverbs 1:8–9

Q. Do you get along with your family? Mine always fights.

A. My brothers and parents and I get along great. We're a normal family. We get frustrated with each other sometimes, but we really enjoy each other's company. We are not big talkers, so we don't argue. We usually have an agenda—like to go find waves—and an argument can put a hold on that.

Q. Do your parents listen to you? Mine won't. They walk away or don't take my question seriously and say, "Don't worry about it." How can I talk to them without them blowing up? Can you help?

A. Go to Jesus. He will always listen to what is in your heart. Ask God to help you say the right thing at the right time. Be sure your parents have a little time to listen to you. Timing is key! Tell your parents that you want to talk. Say "I don't want to fight; I just need you to listen. When I'm done you can tell me what you think." Make sure you keep a clean slate with your parents so you keep the communication open. That means saying you are sorry when you need to. If you show them respect, they will trust you and respect your point of view.

Q. When an accident or something happens in my small town, everybody helps out the family. Did people help you out?

A. They sure did. It was unbelievable! Right after I left the hospital, someone offered the use of their private estate so we could rest away from all the reporters and media that were camping out on our front lawn. When we did get back home, the folks from our church had cleaned the whole house and decorated it with lots of flowers. They brought meals to us every night for a few weeks. On top of that our community all got together and started planning a fundraiser to help with all the medical expenses and for a prosthetic arm and for my future.

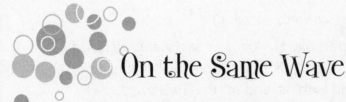

On the Same Wave

Here's what the Bible says about love and unity:

How good and pleasant it is when brothers live together in unity!

—Psalm 133:1

May the God who gives endurance and encouragement give you a spirit of unity among yourselves as you follow Christ Jesus, so that with one heart and mouth you may glorify the God and Father of our Lord Jesus Christ.

—Romans 15:5–6

All of you, live in harmony with one another; be sympathetic, love as brothers, be compassionate and humble.

—1 Peter 3:8

Dear children, let us not love with words or tongue but with actions and in truth.

—1 John 3:18

About Faith

Q. What do you think about God?

A. God is incredible. He loves us and wants all good things for us and all his creation. God wants a personal relationship with us, and for that he's awesome!

Q. How is your relationship with God?

A. I love the Lord so much. He is my best friend, Savior, protector, guide, and more. He is everything to me. I feel very safe knowing that he is watching over me and loving me. I can go to him for everything. It is not easy being me, and I really need to stay focused on following his guidance every day.

Q. When did you become a believer?

Q. Have you always been a Christian or is this something new since you survived the attack?

A. My parents dedicated me to the Lord when I was about two months old! I grew up with a strong knowledge of Jesus and the reality of his love, so I made a commitment to follow him when I was around five years old. Since then, I have followed Christ, grown close to him, and learned to trust him in *every* situation. For some people a traumatic event makes them come to God, but I already believed in and was following God. The attack just made me realize how important it is for people to know God, because in a flash your life can change!

Q. *Do you have daily devotions?*

A. I try to spend time reading and learning from God's Word every day. I talk to him often through prayer. It is important to have a strong prayer life because then you have a life of faith that is active. You get excited about how God is moving and doing things in your life. Devotions help you really see the need to walk in holiness and to keep your heart pure.

One of the biggest challenges in my life is surviving my days without a routine. Every day is pretty much on the fly and constantly changing, so a routine is out of the question. I know most people cannot live that way, and I don't recommend it! But that is the way it goes in the surf world. My routine revolves around the waves, and they are constantly changing. Prayer gives some routine to my days. As soon as a need comes up, we just stop and pray about it and then move on. It keeps my day peaceful.

Q. Do you go to church every Sunday?

A. I go to church on Sunday as often as I can, and I like to go to our youth worship on Saturday nights. If I'm home, I always go. But when I'm away from home, my mom looks in the phone book or online for a local church. We have been to more than six different places that had pastors who surf. It's not that we hold that as a qualification, but it helps us feel more at home. Also, when you are somewhere different and the message speaks right to your heart, you can get really excited knowing God knows right where you are. And that happens a lot! Plus, we get to hear about their outreach ministries and their travels to different surf breaks where they help the locals.

Q. Do people get weird when you start talking about Jesus in an interview or something?

A. Sometimes they get uncomfortable. A lot of times, they try to change the subject. By now most of the media knows that I love Jesus, so if they're uncomfortable, they don't call me anymore!

Q. Are people mean to you because you're famous but still talk about God?

A. About ninety-nine percent are nice, but there are a few people who are insensitive. Mostly I get people asking the same questions over and over again.

Q. Were you ever mad at God for what happened?
Q. Do you ever hate God for letting this happen?

A. No. I have never blamed or felt angry at God for the shark attack. I know that because he loves me, he only wants what is best for me. He promises that when bad things happen, he will make them work out "for the good of those who love him, who have been called according to his purpose" (Romans 8:28). I now believe that more than ever before, because now I can see all the wonderful things that God has done since the attack.

Q. Is your family Christian?

A. Yes. It is wonderful to have their support. And growing up in a Christian family that loves going to church and loves the Word has helped strengthen and grow my relationship with God.

Q. Can God see what I'm doing?

A. God knows and sees everything today and even before the earth was created. He knows the intentions of your heart and what you are thinking. See what the Bible says about this subject.

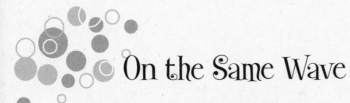

On the Same Wave

Here's what the Bible says about what God knows:

Nothing in all creation is hidden from God's sight. Everything is uncovered and laid bare before the eyes of him to whom we must give account.

—*Hebrews 4:13*

For the eyes of the LORD range throughout the earth to strengthen those whose hearts are fully committed to him.

—*2 Chronicles 16:9*

The LORD searches every heart and understands every motive behind the thoughts.

—*1 Chronicles 28:9*

Q. How do I know God is with me?

Q. God seems so far away. How can I find him?

A. The Word of God (the Bible) states that God will never leave us nor forsake us. He tells us that he will draw near to us when we draw near to him. Spend time reading the Bible and listening to him. Pray before you read and ask the Lord to speak to you through his Word! It is really exciting when I'm reading devotions and it seems to fit exactly what is going on in my life right then. That happens to me a lot. It makes me hungry for more! You'll get to know him through his Word, learn to trust him, and really experience knowing his love and care in your life. God reveals himself to us and speaks to us through the Bible and through our time spent alone with him.

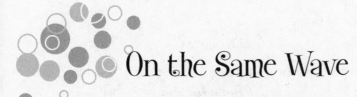

On the Same Wave

**Here's what the Bible says about
God's presence:**

[God] is not far from each one of us.

—Acts 17:27

*Where can I go from your Spirit? Where can I flee from
your presence? If I go up to the heavens, you are
there; if I make my bed in the depths, you are there.
If I rise on the wings of the dawn, if I settle on the
far side of the sea, even there your hand will
guide me, your right hand will hold me fast.*

—Psalm 139:7–10

Q. What's your favorite Bible verse?

A. Oh, that's an easy one—Jeremiah 29:11: " 'For I know the plans I have for you,' declares the LORD, 'plans to prosper you and not to harm you, plans to give you hope and a future.' " That verse really uplifted and inspired me when I was recovering from the attack.

Q. What's your favorite Bible story?

A. David fighting the giant Goliath.

Q. Do you have a favorite person from the Bible? Why that one?

A. Jesus, because he is God in person! And Queen Esther too. She was alone most of the time in her struggles. She had a lot at stake if she blew it, but her faith and love for God helped her to be victorious.

Q. How do you know the Bible is true?

A. I believe the Bible is very accurate from a historical perspective. Archeologists and historians have proven that over and over; for example, there is proof a worldwide flood really happened and that Jesus lived and preached on earth. I also believe that what it teaches us about human behavior, like sinfulness and our need to know God, is true. This truth is played out in the testimony of changed lives after they encounter the living God. The Bible has lasted through thousands of years, and many different people have read its words and believed they're true. The Bible is God's love letter to his people. Plus, I know it is true because it says so right in the Bible. And I trust God to be true to his word.

On the Same Wave

The grass withers and the flowers fall, but the word of our God stands forever.

—*Isaiah 40:8*

For the word of God is living and active. Sharper than any double-edged sword, it penetrates even to dividing soul and spirit, joints and marrow; it judges the thoughts and attitudes of the heart.

—*Hebrews 4:12*

All Scripture is God-breathed and is useful for teaching, rebuking, correcting and training in righteousness.

—*2 Timothy 3:16*

Q. You have inspired me in so many ways. My faith is stronger because of you. One of my goals this year is to read the entire Bible. Have you read the whole Bible?

A. I haven't yet. But I am working on it! I am more of a sporadic reader. On New Year's 2004 I committed to reading the Bible every single day, and I actually pulled it off!

Q. How do I ask for God's help?

A. You just ask him! I pray for God's help all the time. Like when the shark attacked me. I asked God to please help me get back to the beach and to keep me alive. I knew if I could get back to the beach, I had a good chance of staying alive. God answered my prayer that day with a *yes!* Praying is simple; you just speak to God. You can even speak to him through your thoughts!

Q. I heard you're a Christian. If you're so good, why did this happen to you?

A. Sometimes God's plan doesn't make sense to us until we see the later outcome. The attack didn't happen because I was bad or good. It just happened. God wasn't punishing me or anything. I believe God allowed it to happen so he could use me in a special way. That way I can tell others about him. God has a plan. Even though it is hard to understand, trust that he can use even a bad situation for good. He will.

Q. How does God tell you what to do?

A. God talks to us in different ways. If we study the Bible, he will guide us through what we read. He talks through situations or other people, like parents, youth leaders, pastors, or even friends. He talks to us by helping us think of options or solutions to a problem. He guides us through the Holy Spirit, who speaks into our conscience. A lot of times when I'm asking God what to do, I'll read the Bible, and he will speak to me through what I read.

One time my brother Noah took me to pick up a new surfboard. I chose one that was decorated with palm fronds. We thought that it was creative, but it didn't look like it would win any art awards. Then we heard a pastor teach on how Jesus was worshipped with waving palm fronds. Then we recognized that my surfing was like waving a palm frond up and down—and that is a way I honor him! This revelation confirmed to me and my family that we were doing what God wanted us to do!

Q. What does Jesus mean to you?

A. Jesus means everything to me. He created me, gave me life, and saved me from eternal death. He cares for me and loves me no matter what. He is my Savior and Lord, my guide, and my best friend. He rules my life. His goal is to have a relationship with me. He will never leave me or forsake me. He is my peace, my joy, and my comfort. I adore him.

Q. I need your help, Bethany. I used to be a very strong Christian, and then we moved. My mom married someone new, and we never go to church now. I feel far away from God. What can I do?

A. First of all, Christianity extends beyond church to a personal relationship with God on a daily basis. Start by seeking God on your own every day through prayer and reading the Bible. Try to treat others as Christ would. Maybe you can meet other Christians at school who you can go to church with. And talk to your mom and tell her how you feel. Maybe she would like to get back to going to church too. There is really great Christian music out there that will speak to your heart! Search it out like hidden treasure! Keep reading your Bible and praying about this situation. God will help you work it out. He has a plan. He will help you.

Q. Does God answer prayer?

A. Yes! God sure does answer prayer! And I'm alive to tell you about it. He answers in ways that will surprise you and also help you to feel very loved. He may answer your prayers through circumstances or through encounters with people or through his Word. God's Word is alive and can speak to your heart and your situation. It is like a hidden treasure sitting in your lap, waiting to be discovered. He doesn't always answer right away or with a yes, but he always answers. You are his beloved!

Q. What do you pray about?

A. I talk to God about whatever comes to my mind. I am not too formal or organized. I often ask for his protection and care during everyday things and when I travel and surf. I pray for my friends and family and for different needs or situations that concern me. My mom and I also like to pray for people who are having problems that we read about in the newspaper or hear about on the news. I also praise and thank him for each of the things he has done in my life and in my friends' lives. I pray for God's will to be done in my life and for him to give me opportunities to share his love and salvation. And I pray that he would work in my heart and make it more like his.

Q. How do I learn how to pray?

A. Prayer is just talking to God. So, start by having a conversation with God like you would a friend. Talk to him out loud or in your thoughts. What do you talk to him about? Well, the Bible says to come to him humbly and with thanksgiving and repentance.

The acronym ACTS will help you remember what to include in a prayer, so you don't just ask for things when you pray. A is for adoration (praising God). C is for confession (admitting when you sinned and apologizing to God). T is for thanksgiving (thanking God for specific things). S is for supplication (requesting something of God).

Prayer is a two-way conversation; so learn how to listen to God. He will often speak to you when you read the Bible. And sometimes you need to be still and quiet and wait for him to speak to your heart.

On the Same Wave

Here are a few prayers from the Bible:

"This, then, is how you should pray:

'Our Father in heaven, hallowed be your name, your kingdom come, your will be done on earth as it is in heaven. Give us today our daily bread. Forgive us our debts, as we also have forgiven our debtors. And lead us not into temptation, but deliver us from the evil one.' "

—Matthew 6:9–13

Teach me your way, O Lord, and I will walk in your truth; give me an undivided heart, that I may fear your name. I will praise you, O Lord my God, with all my heart; I will glorify your name forever. For great is your love toward me.

—Psalm 86:11–13

Q. How has God answered your prayers?

A. Here's a big one. Just a few weeks before the shark attack, my mom and I started praying for God to use me some way, somehow. Now through the attack and the loss of my arm, he has used me in a way that neither my mom nor I expected. He has used my story to tell people around the world about his love and his care. I've had opportunities to help others and tell them to have courage and not to be afraid. I never would have had those opportunities if that shark had been swimming someplace else. God definitely answers prayers!

Q. How can I make a difference at school and show my faith? There's so much pressure to be popular and attractive.

A. It's hard to be different from everyone else at school, but you need to show others that you are a Christian by what you do and what you say. You can start by being kind to everyone, respecting your teachers, following the rules, playing fair, doing your own homework, being honest, and telling the truth. Those things might sound ordinary, but many kids don't do them. Remember that the tiniest acts of kindness honor God and speak of his love more than you realize! You can also share your testimony and faith in God with others and let them know how much he loves them.

Q. Does God really love me?

Q. How can I get God to love me?

A. God loves you so much that he sent his Son, Jesus, to earth to die for your sins. He created you and has loved you since even before you were born. You don't have to make him love you, because he loved you first and continues to love you even if you have turned your back on him. He wants to have a personal relationship with you. In the Bible, which is God's love letter to us, he tells us over and over how much he loves and cares for us.

On the Same Wave

Here's what the Bible says about God's love for us:

God demonstrates his own love for us in this: While we were still sinners, Christ died for us.

—Romans 5:8

For God so loved the world that he gave his one and only Son, that whoever believes in him shall not perish but have eternal life.

—John 3:16

How great is the love the Father has lavished on us, that we should be called children of God! And that is what we are!

—1 John 3:1

[God] chose us in him before the creation of the world to be holy and blameless in his sight. In love he predestined us to be adopted as his sons through Jesus Christ, in accordance with his pleasure and will.

—Ephesians 1:4–5

How precious to me are your thoughts, O God! How vast is the sum of them! Were I to count them, they would outnumber the grains of sand.

—Psalm 139:17–18

Q. You know what God wants you to do with your life. But I'm not sure about me. What does he want me to do with my life?

A. That's a question almost everybody asks sometime in their lives. It's hard to know exactly what God wants you to do as a lifetime work. Wouldn't it be great if he would just send an email spelling it all out? But he doesn't—he wants you to seek him for the answer.

First you need to check out what kind of gifts you've got, what comes naturally to you, what you are good at. These are gifts that God gave you a desire and passion to use. My mom was a waitress because she loved to serve people and make sure they were well taken care of.

Where you live can affect your life work. Whether you live by the ocean or a mountain or a nature preserve, these natural factors may influence the decisions you make or the skills and passions you develop.

You need to explore your options, try things out, and have a variety of experiences to know what you like to do. Ask for guidance from above, because he can cut a lot of corners and save you a lot of time and hassle! Pray for his will to be done in your life. No matter what we do for our lifetime work, God wants us to be a living testimony of his love for others. We can do that anywhere, anyplace, and anytime.

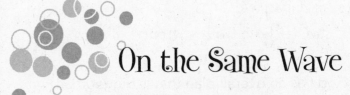

On the Same Wave

Here's what the Bible says about knowing God's will:

Do not conform any longer to the pattern of this world, but be transformed by the renewing of your mind. Then you will be able to test and approve what God's will is—his good, pleasing and perfect will.

—Romans 12:2

[The Lord says:] "You will call upon me and come and pray to me, and I will listen to you. You will seek me and find me when you seek me with all your heart."

—Jeremiah 29:12–13

Be joyful always; pray continually; give thanks in all circumstances, for this is God's will for you in Christ Jesus.

—1 Thessalonians 5:16–18

Teach me to do your will, for you are my God; may your good Spirit lead me on level ground.

—Psalm 143:10

Q. Why does God let things like the shark attack happen to good people?

Q. Why does God let bad things happen to good people?

A. Because God has an overall plan that is bigger than any of our individual lives and our understandings. God uses everything that happens in our lives, good or bad, to fulfill his ultimate plan.

God did not make life this way, with bad stuff happening and sadness and hurt. God made the world perfect in every way, with no pain or suffering or death. But Adam and Eve disobeyed God and sin entered the world. Now pain, hurt, suffering, and death happen to everyone. But God's plan still exists. His plan ultimately benefits those who love him and follow him. So why do bad things happen to good people? He may have a different plan in each case, but I guarantee it is for a much greater purpose than you or I can see.

There's good news too. God sent Jesus to take away the sins of the world. This world has problems. But God promises that one day there will be no more suffering. He will wipe every tear from our eyes. We can receive Jesus and go to heaven. Jesus offers us forgiveness and eternal life. Bad things are only temporary. Heaven is forever.

On the Same Wave

Bad things happened to good people in the Bible too, and God accomplished great things through it.

Joseph was good, but his brothers sold him into slavery. He ended up in Egypt. Years later, here's what he said to his brothers:

"Don't be afraid. Am I in the place of God? You intended to harm me, but God intended it for good to accomplish what is now being done, the saving of many lives."
—Genesis 50:19–20

But no matter what happens, nothing can separate us from God's love.

"For I am convinced that neither death nor life, neither angels nor demons, neither the present nor the future, nor any powers, neither height nor depth, nor anything else in all creation, will be able to separate us from the love of God that is in Christ Jesus our Lord."
—Romans 8:38–39

Q. You say that you do interviews and stuff in order to tell people about Jesus. Has anyone become a Christian because of what you've said?

A. Yes. I've gotten emails and letters from people who say that they decided to follow Jesus when they heard my story. Others have rededicated their lives to Jesus. It is very exciting for me to hear!

Q. Why do you think it is important for you to tell others about Jesus?

A. This is what he has asked Christians to do. I want people to experience God's love and forgiveness. I believe that people are bad by nature. But Jesus died to save us from the result of our sin (death and eternal separation from God). Jesus warns us of hell, and he doesn't lie! People need to realize they're guilty of breaking God's law and have the opportunity to repent and follow Jesus.

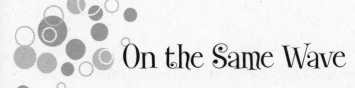

On the Same Wave

Here's what the Bible says about telling others about Jesus:

[Jesus] said to them, "Go into all the world and preach the good news to all creation. Whoever believes and is baptized will be saved."

—Mark 16:15–16

Then Jesus came to them and said, "All authority in heaven and on earth has been given to me. Therefore go and make disciples of all nations, baptizing them in the name of the Father and of the Son and of the Holy Spirit, and teaching them to obey every-thing I have commanded you. And surely I am with you always, to the very end of the age."

—Matthew 28:18–20

Preach the Word; be prepared in season and out of season; correct, rebuke and encourage—with great patience and careful instruction.

—2 Timothy 4:2

School and Other Stuff

Q. Why did you homeschool?

A. A lot of athletes are homeschooled in order to be able to train as much as possible. It was important that I had the flexibility in my schedule to surf when the waves were good, so my school hours needed to be flexible. Homeschooling worked out great for me.

Q. Was your mom a good teacher?

A. My mom was really good with English and Spanish, and my brother Tim helped me with math. My mom knew who to call if I needed help. I only needed to call out for extra help about three times per year.

Q. Did you get a lot of homework?

A. All my work was homework since I was homeschooled! But outside of that, my mom didn't believe in giving me extra work. I just did my regular schoolwork, and then I was done. My mom says extra loads of busywork take away from valuable relationships! She also knew I need to keep up with my Bible studies. I also read a lot of books for pleasure—usually true-life stories of Christians with cool testimonies!

Q. Did you have to take tests?

A. I studied with American School. The tests are at the end of every chapter and are usually six pages long.

Q. I heard you were homeschooled. Did you ever go to regular school?

A. I went to regular school through sixth grade. I attended Hanalei Elementary School. I started homeschooling in seventh grade.

Q. Did your brothers go to regular school?

A. Yes, but they both graduated from high school already.

Q. Do you like to read?

A. I love reading. I read books at home when I am relaxing or to pass time when I am traveling. I also read the Bible every night.

Q. What's your favorite book?

A. The Bible. My other favorites change all the time.

Q. Is reading a nerdy thing to do?

Q. Are you a nerd just because you like to read?

A. I don't think reading is nerdy at all. You can learn so much, and it can be fun! One of the best parts about reading is how you can travel all over the world without leaving your house! You can learn about different cultures in more depth than in a movie. Besides, even if it is nerdy, who cares?! What's wrong with being a nerd? It's fun!

Q. What kind of music do you like?

A. I like to listen to all kinds of music. I really like listening to music that I don't have to be ashamed of since I know God is listening to it too. I like to listen to Christian bands like Relient K, Tree 63, David Crowder Band, Phil Wickham, Falling Up, Switchfoot, Olivia The Band, Something Like Silas, Sara Groves, and Shane and Shane. Not all the songs talk about God, but songs from Christian groups are written from a Christian point of view and don't use swear words or sing about things we don't need to think about.

Q. I listen to all kinds of music — Eminem and Green Day included. I love God. I believe in Jesus too. Is it okay for a Christian to listen to Eminem and Green Day?

A. Just look at the lyrics. If they are bad, don't listen to them. If the lyrics seem clean, then it's between you and God. Every choice we make affects our lives down the road. Just make smart choices on what you listen to.

On the Same Wave

Here's what the Bible says about things of this world:

Whatever is true, whatever is noble, whatever is right, whatever is pure, whatever is lovely, whatever is admirable—if anything is excellent or praiseworthy—- think about such things.

—Philippians 4:8

For you were once darkness, but now you are light in the Lord. Live as children of light (for the fruit of the light consists in all goodness, righteousness and truth) and find out what pleases the Lord. Have nothing to do with the fruitless deeds of darkness, but rather expose them.

—Ephesians 5:8–11

Do not conform any longer to the pattern of this world, but be transformed by the renewing of your mind. Then you will be able to test and approve what God's will is—his good, pleasing and perfect will.

—Romans 12:2

Religion that God our Father accepts as pure and faultless is this: to look after orphans and widows in their distress and to keep oneself from being polluted by the world.

—James 1:27

Q. What's your favorite subject?

A. PE! And English composition.

Q. Do you like to study? Are you a good student?

A. Studying isn't my favorite thing to do, but I like learning so I do it. I think I'm an okay student. I try my best. And I really enjoy learning when it is relevant and interesting!

Q. When did you graduate from high school?

A. In June 2008.

Q. Did you get together with other kids who are home-schooled, or do you do everything on your own?

A. I usually worked on my own. A lot of my friends were homeschooled, but we didn't do homework or projects together because each kid was on a different section, working at his or her own pace. We all did it on our own, but sometimes we called each other for help.

Q. Some kids in my school go around saying my friends and I are stupid, retarded, or freaks. This really hurts kids like me that are trying to enjoy our time as kids. They always seem to walk away laughing. What should I do?

A. It's never fun being picked on! When people say mean things to me, it's hard not to believe what they say. But I know God made us in his image, and he's definitely not a freak, so we must not be either, right? Another thing I do is remember Matthew 5:44, where Jesus tells us to pray for those who hurt us. That might sound like a weird thing to do, but it's possible the bullies are picking on you because they don't know how else to act. God can do amazing things—even work in the lives of bullies. How cool is that?

Q. I hate change. I hate to change grades or schools or teachers. It's just all too scary. You've had so many changes, and you seem to handle it great. How do you do that?

A. You're not alone. Everyone has to go through changes in life. Change can be a little scary, but many times change can be good. God allows change in our lives to help us to grow up. Otherwise we'd still be in diapers! Whenever I face changes in my life, big or small, I trust God that any change is for the best and he has it all worked out.

On the Same Wave

Everything may change, but God doesn't. Here's what the Bible has to say about change:

I the Lord do not change.

—Malachi 3:6

Jesus Christ is the same yesterday and today and forever.

—Hebrews 13:8

Every good and perfect gift is from above, coming down from the Father of the heavenly lights, who does not change like shifting shadows.

—James 1:17

I have set the Lord always before me. Because he is at my right hand, I will not be shaken.

—Psalm 16:8

Q. How can I not get so stressed? Sometimes the homework, my parents, cheerleading, and all the drama that goes on with my friends stresses me out.

A. The best way to handle the stress is to give it to God! Tell him what you are stressed about and ask him to help you find a solution. It also may help to do something physical—like run or ride a bike or surf (my fav). Focusing on getting organized will also help you out. And maybe you just need to cut out some unnecessary activities.

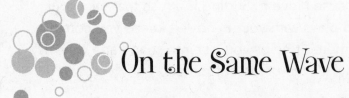# On the Same Wave

Here's what the Bible says about getting stressed out:

Do not be anxious about anything, but in everything, by prayer and petition, with thanksgiving, present your requests to God.

—Philippians 4:6

Cast all your anxiety on him because he cares for you.

—1 Peter 5:7

[Jesus said] "Do not let your hearts be troubled. Trust in God, trust also in me."

—John 14:1

Cast your cares on the Lord and he will sustain you; he will never let the righteous fall.

—Psalm 55:22

The Surfing Scene

Q. Why do you surf?

A. I surf because I love it. Surfing is a rush that stirs your heart and plays with your head—it keeps you coming back for more. It helps you get into shape and tone your body! It's the greatest for me!

Q. Isn't surfing scary?

A. It can be if you surf in big waves. But you can fall and get banged up a bit and hurt doing most anything in an extreme kind of way. I will say that falling into water is a lot easier on you than falling on hard cement or a gym floor.

Q. How did you get so good at surfing?

A. I started surfing very young, and I've loved it so much that it's all I want to do. I practice every day and surf with friends who push me to be better. I also have a surf coach who helps me improve my technique, style, and competition skills.

Q. Is it hard to surf?

A. Surfing isn't easy, especially when you're first learning. It's kind of like learning to ride a bike; it takes time and hard work to learn, but once you get the hang of it and do it all the time, it becomes natural. Each person is different. Some people can get up and ride one of the first waves they try. Others take dozens of tries to stand up and ride a wave. Everybody learns differently. But surfing is so much fun for anyone who tries it, that it's enjoyable just to learn and work at it.

Q. How long and how often do you practice?

Q. How many hours a day do you practice?

A. I surf at least an hour a day. If the waves are good, I usually surf a few times a day, two to three hours at a time. If the waves are really good, I can surf up to seven hours straight. If I'm competing, the entire competition might turn into a practice session, especially if I don't win anything.

Q. What was it like to learn to surf again after the attack?

Q. What was learning to surf with one arm like?

A. At first I wasn't sure I would be able to paddle out or get up on my surfboard. But after a few tries, on three different waves, I got the hang of how to do it. I had to adjust my hand placement and balance before I was able to ride a wave again.

I did have to start out on a bigger board than I was used to, but now I have worked my way down to the size that is right for me. It felt so great. It was a major accomplishment for me. I was thrilled to know I could surf again.

Q. Do you have coaches to teach you how to surf?

A. I have several coaches. My coaches don't really teach me how to surf, because I already know how. They help me improve my style and technique and prepare for contests. Russell Lewis is from Australia. Russell coached me before the attack. He moved back to Australia right before it happened, but he was still able to help me figure out a few techniques that would help me surf with one arm. Then there's Ben Aipa (from Hawaii) who has coached some of the best surfers in the world. He has helped me a lot since the attack. Ben always has a solution for how to do things differently, like visualizing that I still have my other arm when I surf.

My family acts as my coaches too. My dad analyzes the waves and the wind conditions before I surf, and then we discuss my strategy for selecting the best waves. My mom helps me get into my zone. She helps me get my head on straight and stay completely focused—mentally and spiritually. She also prays for my peace of mind during a competition. My brothers help me select which boards to ride, and they encourage me to go on big waves. All of my coaches really encourage me to work hard and keep going no matter what.

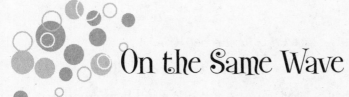

On the Same Wave

Here's what the Bible says about being encouraged:

Be strong and do not give up, for your work will be rewarded.

—*2 Chronicles 15:7*

You hear, O LORD, the desire of the afflicted; you encourage them, and you listen to their cry.

—*Psalm 10:17*

Strengthen the feeble hands, steady the knees that give way; say to those with fearful hearts, "Be strong, do not fear."

—*Isaiah 35:3–4*

Q. I love watching surfer movies. Are surfers really like the way they are in the movies?

A. I don't know. Maybe some surfers are. That depends on if it is a surf video or a Hollywood-inspired corny attempt to capture the surfing lifestyle.

Q. Is surfing good for your health?

Q. Is surfing better for you than other sports?

A. Surfing is great for your health. It's a full-body workout. It's not necessarily better than another sport, but it's still good exercise! Many surfers still surf into their 70s! That is one reason why surf spots get so crowded. No one ever quits!

Q. Do you surf when it rains?

A. Yes, if the waves are good. I'll usually surf when it's cloudy or rainy unless the conditions are dangerous. I won't surf if there is thunder and lightning, or some kind of major storm that makes the waves too wild and the ocean currents too dangerous. Or I won't surf if the rain makes the water murky, because a shark might mistake the movements of a surfer for a fish or seal.

Q. Are you going to become a professional surfer?

A. I hope so! Some people already consider me a professional. But in the surfing world, I'm still an amateur.

Q. How do you stay calm when you compete? I get all freaked out and crazy before a gymnastics competition.

A. Don't be fooled. I get nervous sometimes too. But my family and I pray for God to give me peace and a clear head to be able to focus. I just try to do my best every time.

Q. Have you ever lost a surf contest?

A. Oh sure, lots of times. But I don't let it bother me or stop me from competing again. My mom and dad always taught my brothers and me how to keep a good attitude when we win or lose. They reminded us that sooner or later we would lose, and there's no sense in getting upset about it. It's important to take the focus off yourself and put it on God's plan. I always try to be happy for the person who won and congratulate her, remembering that I will have another chance to compete again.

Q. What's the biggest wave you've ever surfed?

A. It was probably close to fifteen feet high. I'm most comfortable surfing six-footers.

Q. When did you win your first surf contest?

A. I won my first real surf contest when I was eight years old. I won a trophy and two brand-new surfboards. I remember I was really thrilled about winning. It got me hooked on competing!

Q. Do you have a sponsor?

A. I have a couple of sponsors. Rip Curl is my primary surf sponsor. They have sponsored me since before the attack. They take care of all my equipment and clothing that I need for surfing. After the attack, I was really worried that they would drop me, but they were so nice. Steve Cranston from the company flew in from Oahu to visit me in the hospital and tell me that everything would be okay. I have others sponsors too: Claire's, Sambazon, Ford, Subway, Sticky Bumps surf wax, and Surf One Skateboards.

Q. How did you find a sponsor?

A. When I first started competing, my brother Noah created a great letter of introduction for me and mailed it off to various surf companies who make surfboards, clothing, and gear. He worked hard at promoting me and letting companies know that I might become a great surfer. He took photos and set up a website for me. He even created a surfboard design that would be perfect for me. My other brother, Timmy, videotaped me surfing and created little surf videos to send to the companies. My brothers got my name out there and got some companies interested in supporting me.

Q. What does a sponsor do?

A. A sponsor gives you surf gear like surfboards and bathing suits, boardshorts, and rash guards. All the stuff has their name on it so that when you're out surfing, people see that you are using that company's stuff.

Q. You are very motivated to be the best. Who or what is your motivation?

A. I motivate myself to practice, train, work out, and eat right because I love surfing and want to do it well.

Q. Where's your favorite place to surf?

A. At my home breaks on Kauai.

Q. Doesn't the saltwater sting your eyes when you surf?

A. A little. But you get used to it. I don't have my head underwater the whole time!

Q. Do you hate other surfers you compete against?

A. Not at all. I love the girls I compete against. We are all friends, and I pray for them before each contest. Everyone encourages each other and cheers each other on. Ever since I was little I loved the competitions because of all the surfers who got together. Since I surf with different people all over the world, there are always new people to meet.

Q. Have you ever surfed the Pipeline in Hawaii?

A. Yes, I've surfed there about five times. It is normally too crowded to surf on an average day. Pipeline is a very famous surf spot on the north shore of Oahu. I was there in March 2006 for the first all-women's surf competition ever held there. I didn't win or anything, but I got some fun waves, and my friend Alana got first place. I was really proud of her!

Q. Have you ever surfed other places besides Hawaii?

A. Yes. I've surfed in California, New Jersey, Australia, Nicaragua, Indonesia, Western Samoa, Portugal, Thailand, England, Japan, Mexico, and Brazil.

Q. My father said that surfers are wild people and that they do drugs. Do you do drugs?

A. No, I do NOT do drugs. There may be some that do, but there are a lot of surfers who are top-notch athletes, and a lot of Christian surfers who would never dream of doing drugs either.

Q. Do professional surfers make a lot of money?

A. Yes, the best ones do; but it's not a lot compared to what pro golfers, baseball, and football players make!

Q. Do you use a balance board to practice when you're not surfing?

A. Yes. It is fun and helps out with your core balance!

Q. Are there a lot of girl surfers?

A. Yes.

Q. Do all girl surfers wear bikinis?

A. No, some wear one-piece swimsuits, wetsuits, boardshorts, and/or rash guards.

Q. What do you usually wear when you surf?

A. A bikini. Sometimes I wear boardshorts or a rash guard too. And if I'm in freezing cold water, I wear a wetsuit.

Q. How big is your surfboard?

A. I have a bunch of boards, all different sizes ranging from 5'10" to 9 feet. I mostly ride high-performance shortboards (around 6 feet).

Q. What is your surfboard made of?

A. Most surfboards are made with a polyurethane foam and have different kinds of resin to waterproof them. I have some boards made with epoxy, which is a plastic resin, and some made with the traditional polyester resin.

Q. Have you ever thought about teaching at a surf camp?

A. Teaching is more something you do when you retire from surfing! I am not ready for that now! That's something to keep in mind to do in the future.

Actually, I kind of did that when I went to Thailand and taught a group of kids how to surf.

Q. Why do your parents still let you surf?

A. They know how much I love it and that I would not be me if I couldn't surf. They also believe that this is what God wants me to do with my life right now. They live for me to surf as much as I do!

Q. Do you think you will always be a surfer?

A. Probably. I can't imagine life without surfing. I know surfers who are older than my parents who are still surfing.

Q. Do you think you would like to do something else besides surf?

A. No. But if I couldn't surf, I would find something else to enjoy! Where God guides, God provides.

Q. Do surfers really use the word *dude*?

A. Not in Hawaii, but they do in California.

Q. How many surfboards do you own?

A. My family and I probably have about thirty boards all together.

Q. What's your favorite surfboard?

A. That changes all the time. Right now I'm loving my 6'1" round tail.

Q. Do you surf longboard or shortboard?

A. I mostly shortboard. Since that is what I compete on, I almost always practice on a shortboard. I ride a longboard every once in a while for fun.

Q. How many bathing suits do you own?

A. Too many to count off the top of my head! Maybe twenty?

Q. What are some good surfing movies that are okay for kids to watch?

A. *Follow the Leader, Changes, Outsiders, Noah's Arc, Step into Liquid, Endless Summer,* and *Endless Summer II.*

Q. I want to learn more about surfing. Do you know some good books for me to read?

A. One of my favorites that's fun to read (and even mentions me!) is *Surf's Up: The Girl's Guide to Surfing* by Louise Southerden. Some other good ones include *The Encyclopedia of Surfing* by Matt Warshaw, *Girl in the Curl: A Century of Women's Surfing* by Andrea Gabbard, *Surf Diva: A Girl's Guide to Getting Good Waves* by Isabelle and Caroline Tihanyi, and *Surfer Girl: A Guide to the Surfing Life* by Sanoe Lake and Steven Jarrett.

Q. How many surfing contests do you do in a year?

A. At least one contest per month (so twelve each year, sometimes more).

Q. Do surfers you compete with treat you differently 'cause you have only one arm?

Q. Does anyone give you slack during surfing competitions because you only have one arm?

A. No. I'm given the same amount of time in competition to surf as everyone else and I'm judged the same. I don't expect any favors and I refuse them if they are offered. I want to compete fairly, like every other surfer.

The surfers I compete with are competitive, and so am I. Everybody knows I'm serious about surfing and don't expect or ask for any special treatment. So they treat me just like everyone else in competition. One of the nice things about surfing is life is back to normal. I am able to have a surf session and enjoy the waves like I always have.

Q. Do you think having one arm will limit how far you can go in your surfing career?

A. It definitely affects my life in many ways. I might have to adjust how I do a few things, but my coaches, family, and I are sure that if I train hard, I can be a great surfer—and even go pro. Surfing for me is not about bringing home a first-place trophy. It is the ride with friends and family all along the way. The challenge of competition is in my blood, and I do love to take on the strategy of winning contests. It is thrilling to do well—actually a bit addictive—but the real reward is the friendships that you make along the way.

Q. I want to take up surfing. It looks so cool. How do I start?

A. Get a surf lesson from a good surfer who is also an attentive teacher.

Q. I've been surfing for two years and want to go to surf camp. Where should I go?

A. That depends on your surfing skill level. Do a search for surf camps on the Internet or ask at a local surf shop that might have advertisements for surf camps. The Walking on Water Foundation runs some good Christian surf camps each summer too.

Q. I'm going to surf camp soon for the first time. Can you give me some tips or a heads-up about surfing?

A. Don't give up! Surfing isn't always easy, but keep trying and working hard and you'll improve.

Q. I got a surfboard for Christmas. I love surfing, but my sister says I'm a loser and I'll never be a good surfer. Can you help?

A. Don't let your sister get you down. It's great that you found a sport you love. Don't give up. Keep trying. Keep surfing. Prove her wrong.

Q. Do you surf for fun or do you make money doing it?

A. Surfing for me is not about the money; it's about the fun. I make money from my sponsors and by winning a competition here and there, but that's not the reason I surf. I'm definitely a soul surfer.

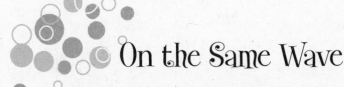

On the Same Wave

Money isn't the most important thing in life. Here's what the Bible says about money:

Do not store up for yourselves treasures on earth, where moth and rust destroy, and where thieves break in and steal. But store up for yourselves treasures in heaven, where moth and rust do not destroy, and where thieves do not break in and steal. For where your treasure is, there your heart will be also.

—Matthew 6:19–21

Do not wear yourself out to get rich; have the wisdom to show restraint.

—Proverbs 23:4

No one can serve two masters. Either he will hate the one and love the other, or he will be devoted to the one and despise the other. You cannot serve both God and Money.

—Matthew 6:24

Q. Have you become a professional surfer yet, or are you still an amateur?

A. In the surfing world, I'm still an amateur. But I'm just starting to compete in professional competitions!

Q. I'm a cheerleader and a gymnast, but I'm just about ready to quit both. I don't enjoy it anymore. It's just not fun like it was. How do you keep surfing fun?

A. I don't have to keep it fun; surfing just *is* fun. I can't explain it. It also helps that I have friends that surf too, so we do it together.

Q. Why do you have to surf so early in the morning?

A. Because that's when the conditions are usually the best and it's less crowded.

Q. How do you know where to go surfing?

Q. Do you surf in the same place every day?

A. Where I surf each day depends on where the swells are and where the waves are good. We pay attention to the surf reports and weather reports. The Internet is a good source for that. My mom and I listen to the local forecast for news about the winds and the tides. We also check the buoy reports that tell about the swell activity. And we call friends to see if they've checked or surfed anywhere yet. Then we decide which surf spots to check. When we get to the beach, I paddle out wherever the waves look best!

Q. I've seen great pictures of you surfing. Who is your photographer?

A. My brother Noah takes most of my still shots. My brother Tim and my parents shoot most of the video.

Q. I'm a Christian surfer too, but I have a terrible fear of sharks. Help! How did you dare get back in the water? That took guts.

A. I focus on surfing and being in God's beautiful creation instead of on what might be swimming in the water. Plus, I think my chances of getting bit again are pretty small. I trust that God is in control. And if I ever feel like I'm in danger, I paddle to the beach immediately.

Q. I surf in Hawaii too. Ever since I read your story, I pray constantly while in the water that a shark won't bite off my arm or leg. How can you even think about getting back in the water?

A. I got back in the water because I couldn't stay out of it. My passion for surfing—what I believe is God's call in my life—caused me to return to the ocean. Like most surfers, I am naturally cautious about sharks. A healthy fear of sharks can save your life. But if you want to surf, you have to take the risk, remembering that shark attacks are rare. Be cautious and aware of the conditions.

On the Same Wave

Here's what the Bible says about not being afraid:

Be strong and courageous. Do not be terrified; do not be discouraged, for the LORD your God will be with you wherever you go.

—Joshua 1:9

The LORD himself goes before you and will be with you; he will never leave you nor forsake you. Do not be afraid; do not be discouraged.

—Deuteronomy 31:8

When I am afraid, I will trust in you.

—Psalm 56:3

Q. Who taught you how to surf?

Q. Have you ever taken surfing lessons, or did you figure it out on your own?

A. My mom and dad taught me how to surf.

Q. What have you done lately with surfing?

A. Check my website at bethanyhamilton.com. Click on the Surfing News page for recent contests and results.

Q. I heard you were a goofy foot surfer. What's that?

A. It's my stance. A goofy foot surfs with her right foot forward and left foot back on the surfboard. The difference between a goofy footer and a regular footer is the same as the difference between someone who is left-handed and someone who is right-handed. It's called goofy because the majority of surfers are regular footed—they surf left foot forward and right foot back.

Q. What's your surf story?

A. My parents put me on a surfboard when I was a toddler. I started surfing at age five. By the time I was seven I could surf and catch waves without my parents' help. My parents started signing me up for surf competitions when I was in grade school. I entered the Rell Sunn contest on Oahu when I was around eight years old. I remember that it was a really big deal for me. And I won! I got trophies and two new surfboards. I was so excited about competing! It was fun and I was really good at it. I've been competing ever since.

In the summer of 2003, I got second place at the NSSA (National Scholastic Surfing Association) National Championship. That October I lost my arm in a shark attack. The following month I returned to surfing, and in January 2004 I returned to competition. I made it to the NSSA National Championship that year—and into the final heat where I took fifth place. But I was so glad to be back.

The year after that, which was 2005, I made it to Nationals again and won the Championship! In 2005, I also got to start competing in a few professional events. I won the O'Neill Pro Junior and got a wild card into the Roxy Pro, but didn't place. In 2006, I also competed in the Target Jr. Pro, Billabong Jr. Pro, Banzai Betty Women's Pipeline Master, and a few more. I made it to the NSSA Nationals but went down in the final. I know there is much more ahead for me. To follow my surfing, go to my website at bethanyhamilton.com and check out the Surfing News.

Q. Since you can't swim with one arm, won't you drown if you fall off your board or a big wave crashes on top of you?

A. I can swim with one arm.

Q. Why do you put wax on a surfboard?

A. Surfers wax their boards to keep their feet from slipping. That might sound funny 'cause when you put wax on other things—like the kitchen floor or a table top—it all gets slippery. But wax on a surfboard is very sticky and keeps your feet in place.

Q. My parents think I'm wasting my time surfing. Do your parents approve of you surfing?

A. Approve? You bet! They're surf nuts just like me. They have been surfing since their early teens, so they understand all about surfing and are passionate about it. They are the ones who got me into surfing.

Q. Do you have to be strong to surf?

A. You have to be strong both physically and mentally for surfing. Your body needs to be strong to be able to paddle out through the strong ocean currents, to get up on the board, and to balance and pivot as you ride a wave in. You need to have endurance. And your mind needs to be strong to focus on what you are doing, to judge when to take a wave, and to know how to maneuver on a wave. It's similar to how we need to be strong to do the tasks God has called us to do.

On the Same Wave

**Our strength comes from God.
Here's what the Bible says
about being strong:**

Be strong in the Lord and in his mighty power.
—Ephesians 6:10

I can do everything through him who gives me strength.
—Philippians 4:13

*[The Lord] gives strength to the weary and increases the
power of the weak.*
—Isaiah 40:29

*The Lord gives strength to his people; the Lord
blesses his people with peace.*
—Psalm 29:11

Q. Do you have any secrets to winning a competition?

A. No, there are no secrets. You have to perfect your technique and keep a positive outlook. Surfing, like many sports, is both physical and mental, especially in competition. Those who are strong in both areas usually are winners. Before a heat, I usually study the waves and plot my strategy. Then I pick out a marker on the beach to line up with and figure out the best place to take off. I sometimes like to surf the spot before the competition too.

Q. Do you always have fun surfing, or are there times when you get frustrated?

A. I sometimes get frustrated when I'm surfing because it is so hard to get good waves. It tends to be overcrowded and everyone is hungry for waves; and I get caught up in that too. But I know how important it is to focus on the eternal things of God and his love, and to keep my heart pure and devoted to him. And that is when I can really enjoy his peace! I like to look ahead at the positive opportunities in life and not hang out in the swamp of depression.

Q. In most surfing movies, surfers appear as beach bums or airheads. How does that make you feel? What is a typical surfer really like?

A. It breaks my heart that movies do that! There are surfers from so many walks of life that you can't really define a typical surfer. Every surfer shares a love for the ocean, the waves, and the thrill of riding a wave.

Living in Hawaii

Q. Is it nice in Hawaii?

Q. Do you like living in Hawaii?

Q. What do you like about living in Hawaii?

A. I love living in Hawaii. It's very lush, green, and colorful. The temperature is almost always warm. It rains a lot in Kauai, but that makes it all so beautiful. I love the sun, the fresh fruit, and the people. There's this spirit of *aloha*, a spirit of love, that is unique to the people of Hawaii. They are warm and loving and happy. It's hard to describe. But it is a special gift from God. I like the flowers, the rainbows, the dolphins, the turtles, and the waves (of course)! I can't think of any place in the world I would rather live. But maybe everyone feels that way about the place they call home.

On the Same Wave

Here's what the Bible says about loving others (in the spirit of aloha):

Dear friends, let us love one another, for love comes from God. Everyone who loves has been born of God and knows God.

—1 John 4:7

[Christ] has given us this command: Whoever loves God must also love his brother.

—1 John 4:21

As we have opportunity, let us do good to all people, especially to those who belong to the family of believers.

—Galatians 6:10

May the Lord make your love increase and overflow for each other and for everyone else, just as ours does for you.

—1 Thessalonians 3:12

Q. Do they have any shopping malls there?

A. We don't have big shopping malls on Kauai.

Q. What do you do for fun in Hawaii, other than surf?

A. Hang out with friends, hike, kayak, go bowling, play tennis or soccer, swim, skateboard, work out, etc. There are a ton of fun, active things to do! I like reading too.

Q. It seems like everybody goes to Hawaii on vacation. Where do you go on vacation if you already live there?

A. Sometimes we go to another part of the island or to another Hawaiian island. Some people go to the mainland or other countries like Samoa, Indonesia, Fiji, Tahiti, New Zealand, or Europe.

Q. It can rain a lot in Kauai. What do you do when it rains?

A. Well, since it rains pretty much every day off and on (at least for a few minutes), my day doesn't really change when the rain starts. I can usually keep doing whatever I was doing when it was sunny! When a rainstorm comes and I can't surf because the water is murky, I try not to be a couch potato. My mom and I like to go look at all the waterfalls when the rain gets really heavy! But I don't really like sitting around all that much. So I do something active or take the opportunity to get a lot of schoolwork done!

Q. Do you speak Hawaiian?

A. A little. Every school in Hawaii teaches the Hawaiian language to students, starting in elementary school. Since I attended public school through grade six, I learned some Hawaiian. Other than that, I know and use the common words and phrases like *aloha, mahalo, pau, hele on, a hui hou, hale, luau, kama'aina, wahine,* and *da kine,* etc. I learned the most words when I was playing ukulele.

Q. Has living in Hawaii affected who you are? If you lived in Colorado, do you think you would be different?

A. Living in Hawaii near the beach with big waves has certainly influenced my love for surfing. I suppose if I had grown up in Colorado, I would be into snowboarding or something like that. But I think if I had been born someplace else, I would still be an athlete of some kind.

Q. I live in a small town and hate it. How do you stand living in a small town and on an island thousands of miles from the mainland?

A. One thing that *is* nice about living in a small town is that everyone knows each other. I think small towns are very friendly that way — it's like one big family. On Kauai, my family and I know lots of people and have friends all over the island. Smallness has advantages: if your car breaks down, chances are that someone you know will come by and help you out and give you a ride home. I think you can make any place you live—large city or small town—fun somehow. There are advantages to living most anywhere. It's all in the way you look at it.

Q. Do people in Hawaii wear grass skirts?

A. Nowadays, Hawaiians only wear grass skirts to perform Tahitian and hula dancing at luaus. Grass skirts are part of ancient traditional Hawaiian dress. Hawaiians wear normal clothes (shorts, T-shirts, tank tops) on a regular basis, like you and me.

Q. What's Hawaiian culture really like?

A. Respect is very important in Hawaiian culture.

Q. Do people in Hawaii speak Hawaiian or English?

A. English and Hawaiian are the two official languages of the state of Hawaii. But Pidgin is used by many locals in everyday conversation. (Pidgin is the language that is formed when several languages mix. Many languages, including Portuguese, Hawaiian, Chinese, Japanese, Spanish, English, and Korean, have influenced Hawaiian Pidgin.)

Q. Does everybody in Hawaii surf?

A. A lot of people surf for fun, but not everybody. Not everyone who lives in Colorado skis. It's the same kind of thing.

Q. What was growing up in Hawaii like?

A. It was so fun! We spent a lot of time at the beach running around in the sand and water with other kids. You wear rubber slippers (flip-flops) or go barefoot most of the time. As a kid, you are taught about respect and showing aloha. You call your parents' friends *Auntie* or *Uncle*. It's a very casual and comfortable place to live.

Q. What's Christmas like in Hawaii?

A. Well, we certainly don't have snow. It's warm here every day of the year, even on Christmas. We sometimes go to church on Christmas Eve. Our family tradition on Christmas morning is to get up early and go surfing, and then come back and open presents. We like to surf then because the waves are usually great that time of year and we have the waves to ourselves—everyone else is home opening their gifts. My mom usually cooks a turkey dinner, and we eat in the late afternoon. My dad usually works Christmas evening at the restaurant, and the rest of us may go surf or hang out together. Our extended family rarely comes to visit for Christmas because they live so far away, and it's expensive to travel during the holidays.

Q. Did your parents always live in Hawaii?

A. No. My parents grew up on the mainland of the United States. My mom lived in California. My dad lived in New Jersey. They both loved surfing and came to Hawaii as young adults to find good waves. They did. They also found each other.

Q. Can you think of something that is uniquely Hawaiian? Something we don't do here on the mainland?

A. There are a lot of things. But one tradition is that you always take off your shoes before you go into the house.

Celebrity Status

Q. Can I have your autograph?

A. Sure. Here it is.

Q. Does it bother you when people stare at you?

A. I think mostly everyone gets annoyed when strangers stare at them. But I'm pretty used to it now.

Q. How many famous people have you met?

A. About 539 ... Just kidding! I have no idea, but quite a few. Famous people aren't much different than you and me.

Q. You've met lots of famous people. Is there somebody you would still like to meet?

A. No.

Q. How many TV shows have you been on? Which ones?

A. I think I've been on over a dozen: ABC Family's *Switched*, *Oprah*, *The Tonight Show* with Jay Leno, *The Early Show*, *Inside Edition*, *20/20*, *Ellen*, *Good Morning America*, *The Today Show*, MTV's *TRL*, *Entertainment Tonight*, *The 700 Club*, *Andaman News* in Thailand, Emme Tomimbang's *Island Moments*, Outdoor Life Network, *CNN Live*, and many others. I'm looking forward to more when the movie comes out! I also did an anti-drug commercial for the state of Hawaii, a Subway Kids commercial, and a Volvo commercial.

Q. What do you think about all the publicity you've gotten since your attack?

A. It's good because I get to share my faith and give people hope and courage through my story.

Q. What do you do when people say mean things or tell lies about you?

A. If they do, then I don't really know about it. Most people are pretty nice. The Bible teaches us how to react in all situations! Pray for them. And I try my best to watch what I say about other people so I don't do the same thing to someone else.

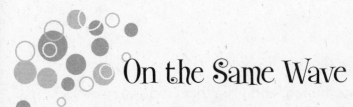

On the Same Wave

Here's what the Bible says about what we say:

Do not let any unwholesome talk come out of your mouths, but only what is helpful for building others up according to their needs, that it may benefit those who listen.

—*Ephesians 4:29*

Do not repay evil with evil or insult with insult, but with blessing, because to this you were called so that you may inherit a blessing.

—*1 Peter 3:9*

Pleasant words are a honeycomb, sweet to the soul and healing to the bones.

—*Proverbs 16:24*

May the words of my mouth and the meditation of my heart be pleasing in your sight, O LORD, my Rock and my Redeemer.

—*Psalm 19:14*

Q. Do you like being famous?

A. Some parts are fun, and I like that God uses me through it. But if I had the choice, I'd choose to be unknown.

Q. What's the best part of being famous?

A. Being used by God.

Q. How do you feel when people tell you that you inspired them?

A. It's surprising! I feel very honored but humbled at the same time, because I know it was Jesus who gave them inspiration and hope; he just used my story.

Q. How do you find the time to write books?

A. Writing does take a lot of time, so I get help from other people to get it all done.

Q. Do you like writing books?

A. I do like writing for the most part—but mostly when I'm finished. It's like when you're writing a paper for school. Sometimes it's hard to write down what's on your mind, but once you finish you feel so accomplished and you appreciate all your hard work. Having books out helps people know more about my story and God. It is a lot of work to tell your story over and over again ... and again! So having a book takes a lot of pressure off me. Like I said before though, I don't do all the writing for my books; I have other people help me.

Q. Did you write the book Soul Surfer yourself, or did you have help?

A. I got help writing that book from a whole group of people, including my family and friends and two writers, who made the work go a lot faster.

Q. How many books do you have? What are the titles?

Q. Have you written any other books since *Soul Surfer*?

A. *Soul Surfer, Devotions for the Soul Surfer, Rise Above, Soul Surfer Bible* (I just wrote some insert pages for that), *Ask Bethany* (that's this book), and a fiction series about me, my friends, and our adventures!

Q. Have people in other countries heard about your book?

A. Yes. The book *Soul Surfer* has been translated into several languages: German, Spanish, and Japanese!

Q. Bethany, you totally rock! Do you ever make public appearances to sign your book or something? When? Where? I want so much to meet you.

Q. Do you ever go around and sign books and stuff? Will you be coming to Seattle soon?

A. My publishers usually like me to do an author tour after a book is released, so I may be appearing in some bookstores around the country. For the latest happenings, check out the calendar on the website, bethanyhamilton.com, to get the latest news on where I'll be. There just might be something going on in a city where you live. You never can tell where I'll show up next!

Q. Do you think you've made a difference in people's lives because you've told your story?

A. I know I have. I get so many letters and emails that say so. And people tell me all the time when they see me. And something that's even more exciting—I know people who have come to believe in God and follow him or rededicate their lives to him because of hearing my story.

Q. Do photographers try to take your picture all the time like they do with movie stars?

A. Not really. Mostly only fans ask to take a picture with me. But the press does it sometimes.

Q. Have you counted how many letters and emails you've received?

A. I'm not keeping track, but my brother has been. According to him, I've gotten over 50,000 letters, emails, and comments on the website message board since 2003.

Q. How do you keep from being scared when you talk in front of a group? I get petrified when I have to give a speech in front of class.

A. It's not that scary for me. I just talk like I'm talking to ten people.

Q. How do you feel when you see yourself on TV?

A. I don't like to watch myself on TV unless I am surfing! *Switched* was by far the most fun show I've ever been on! I enjoyed that, but it wasn't easy.

Q. How do you decide what stuff to do—what competitions to surf in or which place to speak at?

Q. You must have lots of things people want you to do. How do you decide?

A. My dad and my brother Noah help me decide what contests to surf in. But I try to enter all that I can because the more practice I get, the better. As for speaking engagements and appearances, my agent, Roy, and assistant, Becky, narrow down all the requests and present them to my family. Then we pray together and look at our calendar, and decide what our priorities will be.

On the Same Wave

Here's what the Bible says about serving the Lord:

Serve wholeheartedly, as if you were serving the Lord, not men, because you know that the Lord will reward everyone for whatever good he does.

—Ephesians 6:7–8

Each one should use whatever gift he has received to serve others, faithfully administering God's grace in its various forms. If anyone speaks, he should do it as one speaking the very words of God. If anyone serves, he should do it with the strength God provides, so that in all things God may be praised through Jesus Christ.

—1 Peter 4:10–11

We pray this in order that you may live a life worthy of the Lord and may please him in every way: bearing fruit in every good work, growing in the knowledge of God.

—Colossians 1:10

Q. Girls in my school who aren't even close to being famous like you are really stuck up. How do you stay so nice? How do you keep from getting full of yourself?

A. I'm a normal person like anyone else. And the world does not revolve around me. I have been raised since I was a baby to focus all of my love on Jesus, and that love is expressed in how you love others. Jesus taught us in his Word that how you love others is how you love him, and that whatever you do to the least of these you do unto him. So my mom would not allow me to call my brothers any mean names as this would be like calling Jesus a name. Jesus also teaches us to treat others as if they were more important than ourselves. If you take God at his word, then it helps you to be nicer to others and to treat them with respect. Jesus teaches us to have compassion for others.

On the Same Wave

Here's what the Bible says about pride:

Pride goes before destruction, a haughty spirit before a fall.

—Proverbs 16:18

Do not think of yourself more highly than you ought, but rather think of yourself with sober judgment, in accordance with the measure of faith God has given you.

—Romans 12:3

Everyone who exalts himself will be humbled, and he who humbles himself will be exalted.

—Luke 18:14

When pride comes, then comes disgrace, but with humility comes wisdom.

—Proverbs 11:2

Q. When you go someplace to speak or to surf, do you have to travel alone, or do your mom and dad go with you?

A. I usually have someone traveling with me. Sometimes it's my mom, my dad, one of my brothers, or a close friend that comes with me. When I travel for surf competitions, my other friends are usually in the competitions too. There's usually a whole bunch of us, which makes traveling a lot more fun than doing it alone.

Q. Do you mind being called a shark-attack survivor?

A. Not really, because I am a shark-attack survivor, among other things. And that title works better than some names that you have no control over. I'm working on changing the title of survivor to something more positive about what I've done with my surfing career and as a Christian athlete.

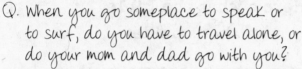

Q. Have you ever ridden in a limo like a movie star does?

A. Yes, I've ridden in a limo. Anyone can ride in a limo. You just have to rent one. I did for the first time in New York City shortly after the attack, right before Christmas. It was fun, but I think it's way overrated. My best ride was a white, super-long Hummer limo with cowboy decorations! That was when my family was invited to Steamboat Springs in Colorado and I learned to snowboard.

Q. What do you think is your biggest success so far?

A. Winning the National Championship in 2005. I won first place in the NSSA Explorer Women's Division.

Q. How many awards have you gotten since you got famous?

A. Here are the honors I've been given since the shark attack in 2003—for surfing and other things. And there were many other events I couldn't attend ... no time!!!!!

Honor Awards:

✦ 1st Pitch Ceremony Award from Oakland A's (2004)

✦ Appointed Chairwoman of the Beating the Odds Foundation (2004)

✦ Appointed Board Member of World Vision International (2004)

+ ESPY Award from ESPN for Best Comeback Athlete (July 2004)

+ Teen Choice Awards—Special Courage Award (August 2004)

+ Wahine O Ke Kai (Woman of the Sea) Award (August 2004)

+ Gene Autry Courage Award (August 2004)

+ United States Sports Academy (USSA) Courage Award (2005)

+ Mildred "Babe" Didrikson Zacharias Courage Award (2005)

+ Free Spirit Award from *USA TODAY* in Washington, DC (2005)

+ 1st Pitch Ceremony Award from New York Yankees (2005)

Surfing Awards:

+ 5th place—National Scholastic Surfing Association (NSSA) Hawaii Event #6 (January 2004)

+ 1st place—Rip Curl's China Wahine Surfing Classic (June 2004)

+ 5th Place—2004 NSSA National Championship Event (June 2004)

+ 1st place—NSSA Hawaii Event #1 (August 2004)

+ 2nd place—NSSA Hawaii Event (January 2005)

+ "Top Finishing Girl" placing 3rd in the Irons Brothers Invitational Expression Session (February 2005)

- ✦ 1st Place—2005 NSSA National Championship Event (June 2005)
- ✦ 2nd place—2006 NSSA Hawaii Event #1 (August 2005)
- ✦ 1st Place—O'Neill Island Girl Junior Pro (September 2005)
- ✦ 2nd place—Roxy Pro Trial: Association of Surfing Professionals (ASP) WCT Women's Event (November 2005)
- ✦ 2nd place—Rip Curl USA Grom Search National Championship (November 2005)
- ✦ 1st place—NSSA/Jamba Juice Event #7 (February 2006)
- ✦ 5th Place—NSSA National Championship Event
- ✦ 2nd place—ASP WCT Women's Event, Australia (April 2006)
- ✦ 2nd place—NSSA Hawaii Event #1 (August 2006)
- ✦ 3rd Place—Billabong Pro Junior (August 2006)

Q. If you stop being famous, what will you do?

A. God has a plan for everyone's life. I know he has a plan for me, so I'm not worried about it. I'll just follow where he wants me to go. One thing is for sure: if it's God's will, I'll keep on surfing. As to all the other stuff, I'll follow where God wants me to go and do what he wants me to do.

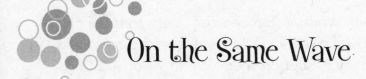

On the Same Wave

Here's what the Bible says about God's plans:

In his heart a man plans his course, but the LORD determines his steps.

—Proverbs 16:9

"For I know the plans I have for you," declares the LORD, "plans to prosper you and not to harm you, plans to give you hope and a future."

—Jeremiah 29:11

It is God who works in you to will and to act according to his good purpose.

—Philippians 2:13

Q. What do you do for World Vision?

A. I work with World Vision because I want to focus on
    the needs of disabled children all over the world and
    raise money to support them. World Vision is a Chris-
    tian organization that helps provide them with care,
    love, and support, and gives them hope through Jesus
    Christ. I want to show the world's needy children that
    God has plans for their lives no matter what challenge
    they face. It's amazing how even a small amount of
    money can go so far to help kids in need.

Q. Why do you do stuff for World Vision?

A. Jesus teaches us to care about others. We were not
    put here to merely exist. As a Christian, I know that
    God wants me to share his love with others. Because I
    am thankful for all he has done for me, I want to be a
    part of what he is doing to care for others, and I want
    to show others that God loves them. God has enabled
    me to help them by supporting and promoting World
    Vision.

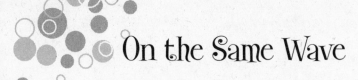

On the Same Wave

Here's what the Bible says about caring for others:

Blessed is he who is kind to the needy.
—Proverbs 14:21

[Jesus said,] "Give to the one who asks you, and do not turn away from the one who wants to borrow from you."
—Matthew 5:42

In everything, do to others what you would have them do to you, for this sums up the Law and the Prophets.
—Matthew 7:12

And if anyone gives even a cup of cold water to one of these little ones because he is my disciple, I tell you the truth, he will certainly not lose his reward.
—Matthew 10:42

For I was hungry and you gave me something to eat, I was thirsty and you gave me something to drink, I was a stranger and you invited me in, I needed clothes and you clothed me, I was sick and you looked after me, I was in prison and you came to visit me.

—Matthew 25:35–36

What's Happening Next?

Q. What have you been up to since the attack several years ago?

A. Trying to get back on track with my surfing, working with my coaches, getting my schoolwork done ... all of this in between media events.

Q. I think you are very brave. How did you get so brave?

A. Practice! Lots of experience! Surfing every day, you want bigger and bigger waves, so the challenges increase and you learn to face them daily one by one. God prepares me through those day-to-day things to face the bigger challenges that will come later.

Q. How do you handle all the pressure on your time?

A. I have my parents and other adults who help me balance everything. I also pray a lot to ask God to tell me what would be the best use of my time. I actually do get behind on things now and then.

Q. Do you ever wish you could just do your own thing and surf as much as you want rather than do interviews and travel and stuff?

A. It is not always going to be like this. Things are settling down to a routine and I am getting to do some really special things and help others too! But I realize that as you get older you have more responsibilities. Doing new and different things can be the fun part of growing up.

Q. Do you ever wish you weren't the center of attention and things were like they were when you were twelve or so?

A. Once in a while I wish my life could be back to normal, the way it once was. But there is something exciting about my life now. I'm a stronger and more well-rounded person because of all that's happened to me. I've learned so much and grown up a lot since then. I know that God inspires me to do all this. It's been really exciting to see what he can do when I step out in faith and let him use me. Besides, everybody grows up. I can't go back to being twelve again.

Q. I think the future is scary. There are just too many decisions to make. How do you look forward to the future?

A. I trust God to love and always care for me, so I have a peace that he will never leave me nor forsake me. And he will guide me each day. My future is in God's hands.

On the Same Wave

Here's what the Bible says about trusting God:

Trust in the Lord with all your heart and lean not on your own understanding; in all your ways acknowledge him, and he will make your paths straight.

—Proverbs 3:5–6

When I am afraid, I will trust in you.

—Psalm 56:3

The Lord is good, a refuge in times of trouble. He cares for those who trust in him.

—Nahum 1:7

The Lord's unfailing love surrounds the man who trusts in him.

—Psalm 32:10

Q. Have you had to change any of your dreams or plans since the attack?

A. There was one thing that I had to give up—playing the guitar. You really can't do that with only one hand. I know that some people play guitar with their feet, but I don't think I'm that good. So I won't play the guitar. But there's so much more that I can do and am doing that I don't think about it. My mom would like me to learn to play her keyboard, but I have really been too busy to take the time for that.

Q. Do you have plans for your career?

A. It's hard for me to make plans since different opportunities come my way every day. I'm just working on doing what God wants me to do and following his lead. Only he knows how to really fulfill us with a future and a hope. My mom says that the people in your future are of more value than your career, so it is important to seek God's will in your relationships and your career. But one thing will always be part of my career plans—surfing.

Wrap-Up

Well gang, hope you enjoyed reading what everyone's been asking me for the past couple of years. And I hope I have answered all of your questions!

One last thing: If you believe in God and have a personal relationship with Jesus Christ, stay close to him and keep following him. If you don't know God personally yet, seek him and you will find him. The Bible promises you that. Check it out in Isaiah 55:6.

God loves you. He will stay by you through everything. I know that my future (and yours too) will be absolutely awesome because God is with us all the way!

May God bless you,

Bethany

May the God of hope fill you with all joy and peace as you trust in him, so that you may overflow with hope by the power of the Holy Spirit.

—Romans 15:13

Rise Above

A 90-Day Devotional

Bethany Hamilton
with Doris Rikkers

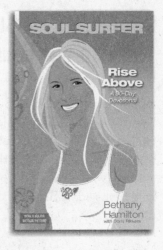

In *Rise Above*, a book of devotions, teen surfing star Bethany Hamilton shares with young girls her courage and enthusiasm for God, inspiring them to face life head-on and stand strong in their faith.

Soul Surfer Bible
With Bethany Hamilton

A companion to the Soul Surfer books, this NIV surfer-style Bible helps girls eight to twelve apply Bethany Hamilton's messages of courage, hope, and faith. This Bible includes twelve full-color inserts that will help teens apply Bethany's mission to their own lives.

Italian Duo-Tone™, Glitter Wave

Available in stores and online!